RED TRAIN

Robert Auletta

I0139600

BROADWAY PLAY PUBLISHING INC
New York
www.broadwayplaypub.com
info@broadwayplaypub.com

First edition: February 2018
I S B N: 978-0-88145-769-8

First published by B P P I in *Plays By Robert Auletta:* September 2004

Book design: Marie Donovan
Page make-up: Adobe InDesign
Typeface: Palatino

CHARACTERS

JAMES RAEGER, *sometimes called Ranger, mid to late thirties. An instructor in the theater department of a large midwestern university.*

REGINE, JAMES'*s wife, early thirties. Very attractive, always impeccably dressed.*

SANDRA TOWNSEND, *called* SANDY, *born and raised in the south; a graduate student in theater history; mid twenties.*

HARRY HARRIS, *a professor in the theater department, early sixties, looks at least five to ten years older. An alcoholic.*

DETECTIVE STONES, *a police officer, late thirties. Served in Vietnam.*

ANNA LEE, *a young theater student, dark hair; loves experimental and outrageous art.*

JERZY, *a theater student;* ANNA LEE'*s boyfriend; came from Poland a few years ago. A professed anarchist.*

LITTLE J, *a theater student; used to be a yippie, did a lot of outrageous things; now deep into his art period.*

DUSTY, *a theater student; does not really like or fit in with the other students; wants to have a financially rewarding career.*

STUDENT SPEAKER, *should be played by the same actor who plays* DUSTY; *committed to the overthrow of the establishment.*

The voice of a police officer

SETTING

Time: 1972-73

Most of the action takes place in or around the large campus of an unnamed state university in the midwest. The various locales include: JAMES *and* REGINE's *apartment in the Lower East Side of New York City; their apartment in the midwest; various places on campus including:* JAMES' *office, the quadrangle, the experimental theater in the university, a rehearsal space, an underground parking garage, etc.; and some off-campus locales that include,* DETECTIVE STONE's *office a farm, the inside of a barn, a road near a cornfield, etc.*

ACT ONE

(*It is past midnight. A monstrous thunder storm is raging.* JAMES *has just entered the bedroom of his apartment. His wife* REGINE *is sleeping in bed. He has just gotten home and is drying himself off with a towel. He seems quite groggy, almost confused in his actions. Now he drops the towel, pulls off his shoes, and while trying to take off his shirt, collapses onto the bed and falls asleep. As he sleeps, we hear some bits of dialogue, that had been spoken between* JAMES *and* DETECIVE STONES *earlier in the evening.*)

JAMES: You're right. I did lie to you, Detective Stones.

STONES: Go on, New York.

JAMES: I was afraid tell you the truth.

STONES: Go on, go on, New York. Tell me the truth.

JAMES: How much I hated her whole goddamned ruling class family! Why, I could barely stand being in the same room with that right wing bitch! How many kids sacrificed for her families' history and honor! And you think that I could have had an affair with her, put my hands on her in some meaningful way….

(*Two large claps of thunder are heard.* JAMES *jumps out of bed and looks wildly about the room.*)

JAMES: What? What is it?

(*We hear a woman's laugh coming from somewhere in the room.*)

JAMES: No! I mean….

SANDY: Yes, I'm afraid, yes. You guessed right, Jimmy! It really is, in one way or another—me.

(She lights a cigarette. We see her face. It's SANDY TOWNSEND. She smiles at JAMES.)

SANDY: I know, I shouldn't smoke. But I just can't seem to kick the habit—no matter what my present status may be.

JAMES: I'm dreaming. Yes, I'm dreaming. Dreams all over the walls, the bed, my mind. Dreaming of you, Sandy.

SANDY: Of course you are. But it's not the same for me. I'm not dreaming at all. I'm totally dreamless these days. All I have now is reality.

JAMES: Sandy, listen, I owe you something. I mean, something that I should tell you…

SANDY: Forget it!

JAMES: The terrible thing that I did.

SANDY: It's fucked up, isn't it, Jimmy? I mean, screwed up beyond our wildest dreams. How'd we manage it, I wonder? *(She laughs a little.)*

(Suddenly JAMES seems totally fatigued, about to collapse.)

JAMES: I don't know what hit us, what, what happened…how it happened…

SANDY: Then go back to sleep, professor. Get your rest. Forget it. I shouldn't have disturbed you like this. *(Glancing at REGINE sleeping in bed.)* Go back to your wife.

JAMES: I haven't slept for days, it seems. Losing control, wandering about, not sure how I got there… Wherever I am. Out behind the barn, perhaps. Looking, just looking…

SANDY: Where we used to meet.

JAMES: Yes, yes. Looking for you!

SANDY: *(Almost to herself)* For that poor poor little 'ol dead girl.

JAMES: You're not dead! I mean… *(He stops.)*

SANDY: Right! Not dead, not quite anyway. Something still going on—like a fire burning around the edges of my personal manuscript; but slowly, very slowly. I can still see the images.

JAMES: Sandy…

(He moves towards her, thinking that he might touch her. Suddenly there is a crash of lightning and thunder. His body shakes.)

JAMES: Oh, my God, my God!

SANDY: Oh, come on, Jimmy, I thought that you didn't believe in Him! An atheist like you! But in times of war, of death, well, then I guess, anything's possible.

JAMES: Yes, anything. You, Sandy, you! *(He is shivering.)*

SANDY: You're trembling. You're shaking. Are you cold? Are you sick? Poor, poor boy. *(She laughs a little. Suddenly she wants to comfort him, touch him, but stops, afraid that she won't be able to manage it.)* Poor James, poor Jim, poor Jimmy, poor Professor Ranger, poor, poor, *(Suddenly…)* Ranger, isn't that what they used to call you when you were a kid? The Lone Ranger! *(She laughs.)* Poor Professor Fucking Ranger! What a laugh! It was all just a laugh, wasn't it?

(A terrible clap of thunder)

SANDY: Incoming fire! Hit the fucking dirt! *(She laughs.)* I'm cursing a lot these days it seems. My bitter bitter tongue. My language deteriorating, just like my poor, my bod…bod… *(She cuts herself off.)* Oh, if they could hear me back home. I mean, my God, would they be shocked! My family would certainly collapse if they could hear me now! *(She laughs a little, then takes a drag of her cigarette. After a second or two she starts coughing.)* Geez, I've gotta stop smoking, really. It's a vile, dirty, habit, and it's just about *(Very southern now)*, just about going to be the complete ruination of my precious health.

JAMES: Listen, Sandy, stay here! Stay here with me! Never leave! Ever, ever! Okay?

SANDY: Go back to your wife. Go back to your life. It's over. Everything's over for me now. But you've still got a chance. So hang in there, Lone Ranger, and see what happens. *(She looks like she is about to leave.)*

JAMES: No, Sandy, listen, just stay and listen…

SANDY: I hated you, the first time I saw you, completely hated you. You know that?

JAMES: I know. But you were wrong, Sandy. Actually we were both wrong. In the beginning our instincts were completely wrong.

SANDY: Did you push me out of the world, Jimmmy? Was it you that did it to me? Tell me the truth. *(Looking into a kind of blankness)* 'Cause I can't remember properly.

(JAMES just stares at SANDY.)

SANDY: Or someone else, or what? Or what?

JAMES: I'll help you, Sandy, whatever you want. If you want revenge, if you want to destroy…me…anything you want.

SANDY: Who knows what I want? *(Pause)* And I'm still mixed up about you too, completely mixed up about you. *(Pause)* Whoever pushed me off the edge of the earth, whoever… Who cares, really! Who cares, anyway!

JAMES: Sandy, I'm just glad you're here. Just seeing you is all that matters to me now.

SANDY: Be careful, be very careful. You seem so alive to me, so tempting, all that flesh and blood.

JAMES: I don't care what happens to me.

SANDY: Yes, my point exactly.

JAMES: Stay with me, Sandy. Stay around forever. We'll figure it out. I'll make room for you in my life.

SANDY: Oh, poor, poor little Lone Ranger. Who's going to help you now? Your guns aren't real, just nickel plated toys. And your horse, poor boy, is only a radio horse.

(Thunder and lightning)

SANDY: It's getting late. See you around campus some time.

JAMES: Don't go, Sandy. The world out there is so dark, so strange and cold without you.

SANDY: Hey, don't knock the dark, James! I like it these days. Feel liberated by it, you might say! *(She laughs.)* Because now I can say and do anything I want. Curse and scream my damn head off! Do it all! Hate my parents and the constraints of this rotten patriarchal society! Just like the rest of those empty headed little coeds out there!

JAMES: Sandy, I didn't, didn't do that to you. Whatever, I didn't...

SANDY: How do you know? You may have forgotten? Trauma or something. I may have driven you right over the edge, and then you just lost it, and... *(She stops.)*

JAMES: Maybe you're right; because on some level I feel guilty. My mind keeps whirling around. But the

answer's there. I know it! Whoever did it...I'll find out.
I will, Sandy. I swear!

SANDY: Maybe there is no answer. Maybe you should
just let me evaporate. And go on with your life. You
wanted me out of your life, didn't you?

JAMES: I thought so. But it wasn't true.

SANDY: As you killed me with your heart, as your heart
turned against me and killed me...

JAMES: Sandy...

SANDY: There's a blot of blood in my head! A blood clot
in my head! Blinding my brain! The end of memory—
the last moments of living life gone from me! I can see
myself dead! But I don't know how it happened! I can
see myself lying in a field, clothes pulled off, torn off,
naked, dead, roped around the neck like an animal. But
what did they, or he, do to me before I was killed? Or
after? And who was it, or they? And why, why...

JAMES: We'll find out. I will.

SANDY: No! Who cares! Don't pay any attention to
me. I'm liberated now, you see, from everything,
and anything. From wars, from death, and from you!
Especially from you!

JAMES: Sandy...

(JAMES *reaches for* SANDY. *She pulls away.*)

SANDY: Why the hell did I come up here to graduate
school anyway? What was wrong with the colleges
down south? And the very pleasant, if somewhat
privileged life that I had the privilege of living down
there? This brave new world. This blazing heart of
America. But instead, the heart was diseased; its
arteries clogged: stuffed with all these vile, snarling,
spoiled children; hating a war that they could not
understand. Hating a country that they could not

fathom! Calling heroes, murderers; calling brave men,
cowards! But they were the cowards, weren't they?
They were the murderers, weren't they? I hated each
and every one of them.

JAMES: No, Sandy, not every one of them. You were
changing, you were…

SANDY: There's something that you've got to
understand: I'm not just dead, Ranger; everybody's
that, sooner or later; but I was murdered, made dead
by murder! I was a beauty queen, won a contest
at seventeen. And look what they did to me! They
savaged my beauty! They trashed it! Left me half
naked, dead in a cornfield, like a sacrifice to some
barbaric deity, like that poor young girl in that
Stravinsky ballet, that girl who was danced to death.
She didn't even have a name, did she? But she was
lucky; she was chosen; she knew that something holy
and terrible had taken hold of her, something beyond
her comprehension, and that she had to submit to it
for the greater good of her tribe. There was something
noble in it for that nameless girl; but not for me; not
what happened to me; my squalid, graceless, useless
end had nothing redeeming about it, nothing. Unless,
unless…

JAMES: What, Sandy? What are you thinking?

SANDY: Unless I was killed for a reason?

JAMES: For what reason?

SANDY: For the war, for Vietnam, killed by someone
who hated me for what I believed in.

JAMES: What's the difference? You're still dead! Gone
from me!

(JAMES *turns away from* SANDY *now. The light begins to
dim on her.*)

SANDY: It would have made a difference, if I was killed for a reason.

JAMES: Anybody could have done it: some pervert grabbed you, walking across campus. Women have been attacked here, abducted, raped here. Right on campus! People say: you come from New York City, you've seen it all. Bullshit! Not like here! Anybody could have done it! Anybody! Me even! In whatever way I kill!

SANDY: Listen, James, there's something I have to tell you, the one thing I know for certain about that moment, that shadow person who killed me, is he loved me. Or thought he did anyway. Because it's the last thing that I felt, or thought I felt, this powerful love! The last thing that I remembered, before my life was cut off: my murderer loved me! *(Pause)* How lovely. What a way to go. In the arms of a lover.

JAMES: Loved you? How could that be? Your killer? No!

SANDY: Or thought he did. It's so clear in my mind now, what the feelings were.

(She touches his face gently. This is the first time that they have been able to touch. The light begins to fade on her.)

SANDY: So absolutely clear.

JAMES: No, Sandy! Stay! Tell me more!

SANDY: There is no more. *(She is gone.)*

(JAMES collapses into a chair, his eyes half closing—it is now like a dream to him. But suddenly his eyes open.)

JAMES: But, Sandy, one thing I forget to tell you— how I betrayed you. Somehow I wasn't able to get it out. Don't you understand—I don't deserve your forgiveness! I deserve the opposite, Sandy. The opposite!

(JAMES *touches his face, where* SANDY *touched him.
Darkness*)

(JAMES' *office. He and* STONES *are present. They're sitting
down.* JAMES' *mind seems to be somewhere else.* STONES *has
just said something to him and he hasn't responded.*)

STONES: I said that I'm Detective Stones. Does that ring
a bell?

JAMES: *(Snapping out of it)* Right, right, of course.
You're the homicide detective, aren't you. The one
investigating this, this…crime.

STONES: Yes. That's me. The homicide detective.
(He smiles slightly.) Murder. It's very different from
anything else, isn't it? Very special, really.

JAMES: Is it?

STONES: A vocation, I believe, when you get down to it.

JAMES: What, murder, you're talking about? To be a
murderer is to have a vocation?

STONES: For some. Serial killers, I suppose. Hit men.
Actually I was thinking about the homicide detective.
For the chosen few, it's a true vocation.

JAMES: Like you, for instance?

STONES: That's right. Like me.

JAMES: It totally engages you, does it?

STONES: Oh, yes, totally, completely. *(A strange smile on
his face)* Are you a religious man?

JAMES: No. Not really.

STONES: Ahh, too bad. You're missing out on a lot, you
know.

JAMES: Are you religious?

STONES: Oh, yes. Finally it came to me. Not without a
struggle, of course. Then one day—a blaze, a fire. I was

consumed. That's religion, you see, in its purest form—
God's truth suddenly overwhelming you.

JAMES: God's truth you say?

STONES: Yes. Nothing is ever the same again.

JAMES: I see.

STONES: *(Staring hard at him)* Do you?

JAMES: What?

STONES: And now I've made it back! The complete
circle. I've returned home, with my heart full of His
truth, His desire. Ready to serve His will.

JAMES: And what is His truth these days?

STONES: Vengeance. The righteous must serve as
instruments of His vengeance.

JAMES: Isn't it more complicated than that?

STONES: No, it isn't. Pay the price and salvation begins.
Don't pay, and, well, you can imagine. *(Pause)* Can't
you? I mean, if you think hard enough about it. What it
entails.

(Silence)

JAMES: So this town is home base, is it?

STONES: Yes. Going right back to my great
grandparents. Simple but violent people. The same the
world over. Poor people trapped between the weight
of the sky, and the rotting earth beneath them. I'm not
saying there wasn't any love. Or milk in the tittie.

JAMES: *(Glancing at his watch, starting to get up)* I'm
sorry, but I have a class in....

STONES: Wait a minute, professor.

JAMES: I'm not a professor.

STONES: No? Then I'm confused. I thought everyone
who taught at the university was a professor.

JAMES: Not me.

STONES: Then what are you?

JAMES: *(Almost as if he were speaking to himself)* I'm a Nothing, a Nobody. The Man Who Never Knew. The Man Who Made Mistakes. The Man who should never have, never have... *(Coming out of it now)* Something like that. Just a humble instructor, really. No big deal. {He tries to laugh it off.}

STONES: Mistakes? There's few who have made more than me. My former situation here becoming more and more intolerable. So I left, and began to wander across the west, the southwest. The dirtiest jobs. The most dangerous work. Finally I ended up in southeast Asia.

JAMES: What were you doing there?

STONES: Working.

JAMES: Were you involved with the war?

STONES: That's right.

JAMES: So you were working for the military?

STONES: No. I was the miliary.

JAMES: But I thought that you said that you were working, that...

STONES: But killing is work, isn't it? Wouldn't you consider it work? Killing people, I mean. Hard, dirty work.

JAMES: Yes. I guess I would. I would consider it work.

STONES: Back breaking work. Only a fool would say that killing isn't work. And what's the military really about anyway? I mean, let's be realistic, and call a spade a spade: a pack of killers with a strictly enforced dress code. *(Smiling)* That's a fact, my friend, and not any sort of demeanment. Since I'm decorated to the eyeballs.

(STONES *reaches into his jacket pocket and pulls out a picture, putting in front of* JAMES. *It is a picture of* SANDY. JAMES *draws back, startled.*)

STONES: She was a beauty, wasn't she? Imagine what kind of degenerate it took to kill her. (*Looking hard at* JAMES) Imagine the type of perverted... (*Suddenly he cries out sharply, as his head jerks back and his eyes start blinking rapidly. It looks like he may be having some sort of seizure.*)

JAMES: Are you alright?

STONES: (*Coming back to himself.*) Sure, sure. Just one of those...flashes.

JAMES: Flashes?

STONES: Images flashing back into my brain—sights that I didn't expect to see. Sometimes it happens. (*Regaining his composure as he looks at the picture and now at* JAMES.) Not a bad thing for a detective, you know. Sometimes gives me a leg up on the situation. You knew her?

JAMES: Just vaguely. A few words here and there. But I can't really say that I knew her.

STONES: (*Putting the picture back into his folder*) How about meeting me at my office, tomorrow, about two thirty? Strictly routine. I talk to everyone, you know. Is that a good time for you?

JAMES: Sure. Fine.

STONES: In the meantime, I'll prepare myself.

JAMES: What?

STONES: A murder, you know, a homicide investigation—one doesn't enter into it lightly. The spirit, the flesh, even, must be prepared. There are ways, methods that you pick up as you go along. That you learn to sharpen and refine. Adios, professor. *(He exits.)*

(Darkness)

(Early evening. JAMES *is walking down a road in the middle of the cornfields. Suddenly he stops walking.)*

JAMES: This is it, isn't it? Where you were killed, Sandy! Yes, here, here! This is where it happened! Why wasn't I able to see it before!

(Now we see SANDY *standing behind* JAMES, *half hidden by the shadows.)*

SANDY: Go away, James. Leave it. Leave this terrible place.

JAMES: Oh, Jeeezzz... *(Starting to turn around)*

SANDY: No! Don't look at me!

JAMES: Alright. *(He stops turning.)* I won't look at you. But I can't leave you either. Not yet. I've been looking for this spot for days and days, Sandy. Wandering around until it gets dark, and then I hear the trains in the distance.

SANDY: Trains? There aren't any trains around here.

JAMES: The red trains that run at night. The red trains running across the prairies. You must have seen them. They look like they're on fire. Heading into the west.

SANDY: Don't come out here anymore, James. Promise me.

*(*JAMES *and* SANDY *continue standing there. It gets dark. Now we hear the shriek of the trains in the distance and see a slash of fire cutting through the darkness.)*

SANDY: You were right, James. There are trains here.

JAMES: Red trains of war. Heading towards the Pacific.

(The train whistle shrieks. Darkness)

(A rehearsal room in the university theater. JERZY, LITTLE J *and* ANNA LEE *come walking on stage. As the scene goes on, we notice* JAMES *off to the side, in the shadows watching them.)*

LITTLE J: Did you see our new teacher? What a character! Man, is he out there!

ANNA LEE: He's a real artist. Did you get a look at his resume? It tells an interesting story. I'm really impressed.

JERZY: He's worked with the criminals, the drug addicts, with the street people—really avant garde stuff, man. This guy's gonna take no shit around here.

LITTLE J: He's going to do it for us! He's going to make it happen for us! He's the man we've been looking for!

ANNA LEE: I wonder why they hired him? Like, I mean this really square, *old* white faculty! Hiring a guy like him. Unbelievable!

LITTLE J: Somebody said his nickname is Ranger, like the Lone Ranger or something.

EVERYBODY: Fucking Ranger! The Lone Fucking Ranger and we've got him! We've got him!

*(*JAMES *steps out of the darkness surprising them. The scene becomes expressionistic, distorted. We are now inside his mind.)*

JAMES: Hey, wait a minute, gang, wait just a minute! I've got to tell you, it's not going to work out. If I come here, a young woman dies! And you don't want that to happen, now do you?

(They can't really understand him, embarrassed, not knowing what to do, they begin to laugh a little)

JAMES: No! It's not funny! I can't come out here! You understand! There's no way, no way that I can come here. Damn you all, anyway! Go to hell! You and your damned theater!

(The students, not knowing what else to do, start to walk off, talking quietly together. JAMES is alone for a few seconds. The sound of the train passing by. Darkness)

(JAMES and REGINE's apartment on the Lower East Side, in New York City. We can still hear the train whistle shrieking faintly in the distance.)

REGINE: Just answer me one thing: are you going to take that job or not?

(JAMES just stares at REGINE.)

REGINE: They offered you the job, didn't they?

JAMES: I'm thinking about it.

REGINE: How long do you have before you have to tell them?

JAMES: They'd like to hear from me by next week.

REGINE: Well? You sound somewhat less than enthused.

JAMES: You see, Regine, New York City, is my hometown, born and raised here, and....

REGINE: So you're telling me you're not going to take the job?

JAMES: I think I'm afraid, Regine.

REGINE: Afraid? What are you afraid of, James?

JAMES: The war, the people—things are different out there. There's a certain uneasiness. I think it would be a big mistake to go.

(REGINE just stares at JAMES.)

JAMES: Personally, I feel safer here, better off here, working with my drug addicts and ex-cons. You know what I mean?

REGINE: No, I don't. Because I don't feel safe here at all.

JAMES: Look, it's not forever, it's just for...

REGINE: It's not that I don't love it here, James; it's that I hate it here, in this hellish city where you planted us, on the Lower East Side of America. In fact, I think I may be slowly losing my mind, my grip.

JAMES: But, listen Re...

REGINE: No! I won't! There's not enough money! There's not enough protection from the horrors of the world! And in the eyes of my family, my life is nothing but a travesty, a...

JAMES: You're talking about your mother, aren't you?

REGINE: She thinks the life we live here is demeaning to me.

JAMES: And to her as well, I'll bet.

REGINE: There's a grain of truth in what she says. *(Pause)* You got me pregnant.

JAMES: It wasn't rape.

REGINE: Who knows what really happened? Who knows what men are really doing to women these days?

JAMES: Are you serious? What are you talking about? What I've done? What about you?

REGINE: Of course I'm serious! I feel that I might have been raped. I haven't sorted it all out yet, James, but I do know this: you were involved in that moment, but I wasn't. My will was man-handled, overpowered; my body unable to defend itself. And that's a form of rape, isn't it?

JAMES: No. I don't think so.

REGINE: *(Going deep into herself now)* You made me give up my studies, my graduate work. It all happened so

fast. You have a crush on someone. A few dates. Your
head whirls. There are kisses. Where are the defenses?
Where is the real understanding? Women are trapped.
Its pathetic. Brains have been damaged in infancy.
You may be a strong person, but that's not enough—
because you have no idea of what you're really up
against! The invisible, terrible murmurs, the deadly
dreams that destroy women every day.

JAMES: But, Regine, I can't do much about what you've
just said. I don't have any real power either. I'm
trapped in everything as much as you are.

REGINE: *(Deeper than ever in herself.)* You walk around.
You want to have a good time. You just want to be
normal. But, it's not real, it's only a movie. Your life
is only a movie. And it's never been real. Never! And
you don't know what to do about it either. Because
no one has ever helped you. So you look around for
help; you look towards men; because they have most
of the power. So your throw yourself at their feet. But
you soon find out how diabolical they can be in their
niceness, their warmth, their sweetness. The way they
look at you in the moonlight, hold your hand in the
movies. Nothing is what it seems. One too many kisses,
and you've lost your entire life.

JAMES: But, you said that you didn't want to go back to
school, that you were no longer interested.

REGINE: It wasn't true.

JAMES: But how can I know what's true with you,
Regine, if you tell me the exact opposite?

REGINE: I don't have an easy answer for that.

JAMES: Great. That's just what I needed to hear.

REGINE: Okay. Then I'll help you out, James: I want to
get out of this hole now!

JAMES: I have a theater here, a grant. I have another year left. We're able to live, we're able to…

REGINE: I want to get out of this rotten hole right now!

JAMES: I have projects to finish.

REGINE: You do theater for drug addicts, criminals. People nobody cares about. It's not that I don't care about them. I feel sorry for them. But what kind of life is it for me, for your son? Face it, it's a disaster, a complete disaster.

JAMES: I do the kind of theater that I love, with people who have suffered, and have something to tell the world.

REGINE: Yes, you and your art—pardon me while I genuflect. There's another world out there, too—a world that you seem completely oblivious to!

JAMES: Listen, Regine, I've made up my mind. We're going to stay here. At least until my grant runs out.

REGINE: No! I want to go someplace where it's white. Somewhere more abstract. White and abstract. With plenty of large supermarkets. And people wearing clean nondescript clothes.

JAMES: I don't think so. (*He starts to leave.*)

REGINE: You take the job!

JAMES: Why? Even if we go out there, how can I be sure that things will change between us, Regine?

REGINE: Things can get better.

JAMES: But there's no guarantee, is there?

REGINE: Let me have some space, some air, some sky and clouds. A nice clean safe place to live, is all I'm asking. Is that too much to expect? I'm just trying to survive, James. That's all.

JAMES: Tell me, Regine. Just one thing. Is there still love between us? Can that still be hoped for?

REGINE: You take the job. Tell them you really want it. We'll go out there and start a real life. You'll see.

JAMES: Denny will love it. I mean, lots of space to crash around in, animals and stuff. He'll freak.

REGINE: He'll run around like crazy.

JAMES: *(Laughing)* So many opportunities for mayhem.

REGINE: He'll be bowled over.

JAMES: It's sounds good, but…I have to think about it.

REGINE: No, thinking, James! No thinking! Thinking has never worked for us, James!

JAMES: Let me tell you, Regine: I always thought that I could go anywhere, really anywhere, and make sense of it. And make something good come out of it…

REGINE: Then here's your opportunity.

JAMES: But not this place.

(The lightning changes. HARRY HARRIS appears in the distance, quite drunk. The scene is a cocktail party that the theater faculty gave for JAMES in the midwest. REGINE cannot see him. JAMES turns towards HARRIS. The whole effect is suddenly quite surreal.)

HARRIS: Hey, James, Jim Raeger! I've heard all about you. Lot's of excitement, lots of good talk circulating. So nice to finally meet you, fellow. I'm Harry Harris. You're from New York, I hear. Fantastic place, let me tell you. I always have a great time there. The Bronx is up, the Battery down. Or is the Bronx simply upside down, and the Battery completely rundown? Don't get me wrong, I love New York. The last time I was there, well, I had carnal relations with a Carmelite nun; or was it calming relations with a Carnalite nun? Or was it, I was eating caramels with a Puerto Rican hooker on Ninth Ave? *(Laughs)* So hard to remember, but so much fun, really. And, as usual, I went out in a blaze of Broadway glory!

*(*JAMES *turns back to* REGINE. HARRIS *remains where he is.)*

JAMES: Truthfully, this place kind of scares me, Regine.

REGINE: *(Smiling)* A college in the midwest scares you?

JAMES: Yes. It does.

HARRIS: Hey, you're not a Catholic, are you? I mean, I don't want to offend. But if I did, what the hell, because there's not much you can do about it anyway, now is there? I'm a tenured professor, you see. *(He laughs.)* Will miracles never cease! Hallelujah! *(Sotto voce)* It's take a fucking A-Bomb to get me the hell out of there! *(He laughs.)* And don't think they haven't tried! *(He walks off into the darkness whistling* Give My Regards to Broadway.*)*

REGINE: Stop worrying so much.

JAMES: But... Yeah, yeah. Sure. But you see... *(Suddenly he seems groggy, almost on the verge of collapsing.)* I think I'm wrong, not doing a very good job, not standing up for...what I believe. Just a lost, a lost...

REGINE: What's the matter, James? What's happening to you?

JAMES: Vapors, sheets of napalm, floating gently, like clouds across the prairies. Everything burning. The red train. And the girl lying dead in the fields.

REGINE: I'm sorry, James, but I don't understand a word that you're saying. Not a word.

*(*REGINE *exits.* JAMES *stands there alone, as the lights fall into darkness.)*

(The lights start to come up. In the background we can hear a very scratchy recording of Stravinsky's Le Sacre du Printemos; *the volume grows louder and louder, until the*

lights are fully up, then the music stops. JAMES *is standing in a small theater talking to* DUSTY, *who is playing Pentheus in their production based on* The Bacchae. *He's just given him some directions. Now* DUSTY *goes off into the darkness.* JAMES *calls out.)*

JAMES: Okay. Now! That's it! Now get him!

(We hear a cacophony of cries and howls, as JERZY, ANNA LEE, *and* LITTLE J *race on stage.)*

JAMES: *(Pointing them in different directions)* He's there! There, there he is! No! It was an illusion! A shadow! There he goes, there! Now he's there! Get him, get him!

(The three actors run through the darkness, pursuing Dusty; finally they trap him backstage. Terrible cries and triumphant screams are heard.)

JAMES: Yes, yes! Do what you have to do! Tear him apart! Yes, yes! Do it, do it! Kill the tyrant! Kill him! Yes! Free yourselves from the tyrant!

(More bloodcurdling screams, silence, and after a few moments all four actors emerge.)

JAMES: So how did it go? Tell me, what did it feel like?

LITTLE J: Terrible, horrible, really.

JERZY: Oh, man, shit, you shoulda seen his eyes. These stupid pleading eyes gaping at me.

DUSTY: Well, they wanted to kill me, didn't they? I had to do something, didn't I?

JAMES: And what was going on in your mind, Anna Lee?

ANNA LEE: Just really wanting to kill him is all I was thinking about. I mean, what is he but a two bit dictator, a crummy fascist! He laughed at Dionysus, then imprisoned him. Imprisoned a god, can you believe it! An asshole like that Pentheus deserves to die!

JERZY: He reminded me of that fat-Chicago, pig-face, that stinking Mayor Daley.

DUSTY: Oink, oink, sure. But try and see it from his point of view, okay? He did what he thought was right. Dionysus represents anarchy to him and...

ANNA LEE: Who cares! *(To* JAMES*)* Maybe we should be allowed to torture him a little bit before we kill him?

JAMES: No, no. That's not what it's about at all; it's about energy; great fields of pure energy opposing one another.

LITTLE J: Yeah, I can get into the energy, man, but when it comes to the killing, I kind of had to look the other way. Kind of not watch me doing what I was doing.

JERZY: Yeah, yeah, energy, dudes, it's fucking great. What life is all about. Like in Cracow, with our famous underground rock 'n roll band man, the Gin Cats.

ANNA LEE: Oh, man! Cracow, Cracow! I'd love to go there! Take me there, Jerzy! Take me now!

(The lights start to dim. The actors walk off together. JAMES *stands there watching.)*

(The lighting starts to change, signaling a breakdown in JAMES' *reality.)*

JAMES: We'll make them sit up and take notice! We'll make them feel something! Won't we? And everything will turn out alright! Won't it, Regine? Yes, yes! At least we can hope! Can't we, Regine, can't we? We can hope!

(Now we see REGINE, *vaguely outlined in the shadows, watching him. Then darkness)*

(The lights come back up. We now see and hear the end of the play that JAMES *and the students have been rehearsing. The lights are now theatrical, colorful; the sound score is vibrant, alive, filled with echoes of Stravinsky's* Le Sacre

du Printemps, *but done with bells, whistles, drums, etc.*
And now the actors, ANNA LEE, LITTLE J, *and* JERZY,
suddenly appear on stage, dancing and shouting in joy, as
they brandish the bloody parts of Pentheus' body above their
heads. Darkness)

(The lights come back up. The sounds of Le Sacre du
Printemps *can be heard in the background, then fade away*
as HARRIS *enters—only somewhat drunk, since it's still*
early in the day—holding his ubiquitous whiskey filled coffee
cup.)

HARRIS: Well, James. Let me congratulate you. You
did it! You really have. You've reached us. *Fragments*
of the Mother. Mother America was it? Yes, yes.
Crude, but very effective. So what did we have there,
this interesting brew you put together: some Greek
tragedy, the Bacchae, of course, Artaud, and some
poets, mmmm....

JAMES: Allen Ginsberg.

HARRIS: Allen Ginsberg! That's right. How could I
have forgotten? Possibly the worst American poet of
his generation. And a practicing homo, to boot. But he
feels things, I suppose. Or at least he thinks he does.
So let's give him some credit for trying. *(He laughs.)* So
what do you want, James, I mean, you personally, for
us to go home and hate ourselves, because we were
unlucky enough to be born in America?

JAMES: No. But to become aware that there's, perhaps, a
tragic dimension to being an American.

HARRIS: I should tell you something, some people find
this, this play of yours, well, quite offensive. There's
been a lot of pretty intense, pretty angry talk about it.

JAMES: And what about you, Harry? Is that the way
you feel, offended, angry, whatever?

HARRIS: *(Laughs)* Me? No. Not at all! Not-at-all! You see what I concentrate on, is the word experimental; and somehow that makes it okay, as far as I'm concerned. That's why we brought you out here, didn't we, to shake us up, to ex— *(Growling)* —perrrrrr-ii-ment. Right? And that's what you're doing, isn't it? Your job, as you see fit. Experimenting. Seeing how far you might go. How much the social climate can take, before it explodes. Or what the students can handle, before they crack up. Am I right?

JAMES: Thanks for the support, Harry.

HARRIS: So just keep it up, James, that fine challenging work of yours. As long as you can.

(HARRIS starts to walk off. JAMES stands there. The stage darkens. Then a sudden high pitched piercing, microphone sound is heard. The lights flash, sputter, blaze in a weird, short circuit kind of way. Now we see the student SPEAKER, microphone in hand, an American flag outlined behind him. As the SPEAKER speaks large chunks of his words are distorted by feedback, static, or the noise of the crowd. James watches him from a distance.)

SPEAKER: To hell with them! How many more of us have to… *(Noise)* How much blood has to… *(Noise)* Before those fucking Nazis, those Fascists that rule us are oblit… *(Noise)*

(Now SANDY enters on the opposite side of the stage, watching the SPEAKER. This is the living SANDY; she's no longer a ghost. Suddenly JAMES sees her; he doesn't move, but stands there fascinated, watching her.)

SPEAKER: How much longer can we let… *(Noise)* Jackson State! Kent State! How much longer can we allow… *(Noise)* It doesn't take a weather man to… *(Noise of the crowd)*

SANDY: *(Calling out)* Asshole! Go home to your mother, you little jerk! Get your diapers changed!

JAMES: *(Calling out to her)* Sandy!

(SANDY doesn't hear JAMES. He tries to get to her, but is having difficulty pushing through the crowd.)

SANDY: *(Getting into an argument with someone in the crowd)* Yeah. You really believe that? Good. Because than that makes you an even bigger jerk than that jerk up there with the microphone! *(She gives the guy the finger and starts to go off.)*

JAMES: Sandy! Wait! *(He tries to reach her, to get through the crowd, but he can't make it. She's gone now.)* Sandy!

SPEAKER: They bombed Cambodia! And now we'll bomb them! And now we'll bomb them! And now we'll bomb them! And now we'll blow them to...

(A deafening noise, almost like an explosion—the crowd, the microphone? Then darkness. In the distance, we hear the sound of the train whistle, and see the burning glow of the cars as they speed by. JAMES is free of the crowd now, running frantically after SANDY.)

JAMES: Sandy, wait!

(Darkness)

(JAMES is sitting down in STONES' office. He seems confused, not exactly sure where he is, or what has been said to him. STONES has just asked him if he had any reason to want to kill Sandra Townsend.)

STONES: It's a simple question. So why not try and give me a simple answer?

JAMES: *(Suddenly focusing)* What the fuck, you just said to me, that, if I had any reason, to want, to want to...

STONES: *(Cutting him off)* Don't curse here!

JAMES: Here, here, in a police station? You can't curse in a fucking police station? Then where the hell...

STONES: Not at the beginning of a homicide investigation! That never happens here! Not when I'm in charge!

(Note: as this scene progresses, it should become more and more clear that STONES possesses some real power, some strange energy that powerfully affects JAMES, disorienting and confusing him.)

JAMES: I thought that this was just a routine questioning, and now you're treating me like I'm some sort of a suspect.

STONES: I suggest that you give your situation some serious thought and also, that you start to purify your mind.

JAMES: I'm afraid that this is just about as pure as it gets.

STONES: You hope to survive your ordeal intact, don't you?

JAMES: My ordeal! What ordeal are you talking about?

STONES: A murder investigation is always an ordeal, for all concerned.

JAMES: Not for me, because I'm not concerned.

STONES: Guilty or innocent, it doesn't matter; you're now part of something much larger than yourself, New York.

JAMES: Guilty or innocent? I mean, what the hell are you saying?

STONES: I simply asked you if you had any reason to kill Sandra Townsend, and then you lost it.

JAMES: Of course I lost it. I thought I was just down here for routine questioning.

STONES: You mean, you actually had no idea that you were our prime suspect?

JAMES: I, I... You can't keep me here. I'm leaving. *(He starts to get up.)*

STONES: Try it, alright. Just try it. That's all you have to do. Simply try and break free of my constraints.

JAMES: *(On his feet)* I'll try it when I want to, when I'm ready. *(He sits down.)*

STONES: Tell me. Are you a Jew?

JAMES: What? You asked me, am I a Jew? Is that what you said?

STONES: Yes, that's what I asked. Are you a Jew? It's a good thing for me to know, at the get-go, if you're a Jew or not.

JAMES: Why, why is this such a good thing for you to know, at the get-go?

STONES: *(Softly)* Because Jewish doctors kill Christian babies.

JAMES: Oh, shit, Stones! Come on! I can't believe it, man.

STONES: Can't believe what?

JAMES: Tell me, Stones, are you a Nazi? It's something that I want to get straight at the get-go.

STONES: Just trying to get a rise out of you. Just trying to see where you're coming from. Out of what hole or other.

JAMES: So now I'm part of some sub-human species, am I?

STONES: That remains to be seen.

JAMES: I want a new investigator.

STONES: You'll never get one. In this county, I am the homicide department.

JAMES: I won't be investigated by a lunatic.

STONES: But I'm fair. I don't lie, cheat, or falsify evidence, like those boys in blue back in your hometown, are known to do. There's only one thing you have to be careful of.

JAMES: What's that, Stones?

STONES: Do me dirt, befoul me with lies: And I will gather you, and blow upon you in the fire of my wrath, and ye shall be melted in the midst thereof. As silver is melted in the midst of the furnace, so shall ye be melted.

JAMES: Wow. Are you really going to do that? Sounds cool.

STONES: Only if I'm forced to. *(Glancing at a notebook)* So tell me; in your office, at approximately three P M, on Tuesday, April twenty-second, it seems that you had a violent fight with Sandra Townsend, concerning her reaction to that anti-American play of yours—fact or fiction?

JAMES: I... What? Fiction! Goddamned fiction!

STONES: There were witnesses. Lots of people heard what was going on. You threatened to kill her. Fact or fiction?

JAMES: I never, I didn't, I...no!

STONES: *(Begins looking at a notebook)* That you called her a bitch, a spoiled little bitch, who didn't know anything about art, or life, and that someday somebody should shut her up, really shut her up, that somebody...

JAMES: Ok. We had a fight. She has a bitchy mouth. It was just a stupid argument.

STONES: No, New York, it was much worse than just a stupid argument. *(He begins to read.)* "It was really scary. The door to his office was partly open. I couldn't help hearing. He seemed to be losing it. Pounding his fist on something. 'You're dead meat, harassing me like this!' "he said," 'You little right wing C-U-N-, you damned…'"

JAMES: You little right wind, C-U…! I never use that word! I don't use that word! Who gave you that statement?

STONES: I can't tell you that. But here it is: "you little right wing C-U-N-."

JAMES: Cunt! Call the word what it is! You're accusing me of murder, so call a cunt a cunt, Detective Stones!

STONES: Shut up, New York!

JAMES: Who are you, to tell me to shut up, to think you have the right to break into my mind, to say vile things, to ask me if I'm a….

STONES: You're right!

JAMES: What?

STONES: You're absolutely right! I heartily apologize. I really do. Because, you see, there are often times in the heat of an investigation when I'm overpowered, taken over by certain forces, essential forces and powers that I have little or no control over. Powers that care very little for the niceties of procedure.

JAMES: What are you talking about, Detective Stones?

STONES: It was in Nam, the origin of the dilemma, the origin of the species, where these powers first reached me. After this murderous episode. Everybody slaughtered except me. Wandering in a black field of carnage. My body howling like an animal. Wishing that I too were dead! And then I saw it coming towards me.

JAMES: Saw what?

STONES: At first I thought it was napalm, a wave of it rolling gently across the field. And I wanted it, welcomed it, opened my arms to it! But it wasn't napalm at all. It was an angel! The Lord's angel! Burning brighter than any fire that I had ever seen. And then I knelt before it, and it put its hands upon me, and my body began to convulse and cry out, as the Lord's gifts poured into me, His terrible gifts flooding my heart and spirit. Healing my wounds, body and soul, with His power. *(He gets to his feet.)* And giving me gifts, such amazing gifts. Let me sho…

JAMES: *(Getting quickly to his feet and moving away from him)* No!

STONES: Vision and power, vision and power! The vision to see evil! And the power to destroy it!

JAMES: And that gives you the right to persecute me? To…

STONES: Yes! *(Suddenly he grabs hold of JAMES, his arms tight around his shoulders.)* In order to destroy the evil inside you! I'll do anything!

(JAMES' body begins to shake and convulse, as some sort of fierce energy assaults him.)

STONES: You can't resist it! You can't resist the truth of it, can you!

JAMES: *(Struggling)* Yes, yes, I can, I can!

STONES: The truth is in you! Now speak the truth! Save yourself by speaking the truth!

JAMES: I won't be your victim! *(He breaks away from him.)*

STONES: Of course not! Never my victim, never be my victim! Instead, you'll be my brother. Come, now pray with me, brother. Pray, brother! Please, pray with me! *(He reaches out towards him.)*

(JAMES pulls back.)

JAMES: No. I don't pray. I won't pray.

STONES: I didn't want to see what I saw in you yesterday. But I couldn't help it.

JAMES: What? What did you see?

STONES: The spirit of the dead girl inside you, following you. The spirit of the girl you killed.

JAMES: You saw her?

STONES: How you loved and hated her; adored and murdered her.

JAMES: She was an extraordinary young woman. You have no idea.

STONES: I do, I do. Now tell Him, brother, tell Him through me, what you did. Go ahead, speak the truth of your heart, dear brother. To Him, through me. The truth of your murdering heart!

(STONES kneels down and then JAMES.)

STONES:That you killed her, how you killed her, that night, what you did to her. So her spirit can rest.

JAMES: She has to rest, doesn't she?

STONES: You both do. Now tell me. *(He takes out a tape recorder from his pocket and turns it on.)* Tell me everything.

JAMES: *(Thinking for a moment, then…)* No!

(JAMES jumps to his feet and begins running towards the door. STONES cuts him off.)

STONES: You have to get through me first, Brother.

JAMES: I will. I can!

(JAMES *rushes at* STONES. *The two of them grapple for a few moments, until* STONES *spins him around, then getting him in a choke hold, begins to apply pressure.* JAMES *tries to struggle but soon finds himself helpless, barely able to breathe.*)

STONES: I could kill you, and it wouldn't really matter, would it? Because you would rather die then confess, wouldn't you? I could kill you, and my conscience would not be troubled, because I know that you're guilty. But the Angel inside me would not let me rest if I did that, because it wants me to save your soul. But for that to happen you must confess, brother. And you will, sooner or later, believe me—to kill the pain! To destroy the demons! To get me out of your life.

(STONES *let's go of* JAMES *who sinks to the ground, desperate for breath.* STONES *bows his head in prayer. The lights begin to dim on* STONES *and the police station. Darkness*)

(JAMES *is now standing outside the station. It is early evening, the sky laced with burning vapors of light and darkness. Now we hear* SANDY's *voice coming from somewhere in the darkness.*)

SANDY: Run, Ranger, run! Run now, run! Get into your Mustang, your black Mustang, and run Ranger! O Lone, Lone Ranger, run away from it all! Run, now, run!

JAMES: Yes, yes, Sandy. I have to. I will. (*But he cannot move.*)

SANDY: Into the sunset. Hide in the sunset, O Lone, Lone Ranger. Hide there, hide there! And wait for me!

JAMES: Yes, yes, I will. (*He still doesn't move.*)

(Now we hear the whistle of the red train in the distance. The sound of the whistle growing closer each second. Now we see the lights of the train bearing down on him.)

SANDY: *(Crying out)* Run, Ranger! Run, Ranger, run!

(The cry of the whistle, the terrible shriek of the brakes, as the train bears down on JAMES, *who, unable to move, remains standing there. Darkness)*

END OF ACT ONE

ACT TWO

(The lights come up on the theater students. They are in a rehearsal room. There is a fight going on between DUSTY *and* JERZY. DUSTY *has just thrown a couple of punches at* JERZY. JERZY *is retreating.* ANNA LEE *and* LITTLE J *are watching.)*

LITTLE J: Come on guys, let's cool it! Come on, come on. This isn't right! Hey, come on, guys, let's just...

*(*DUSTY *has* JERZY *cornered. He punches him in the ribs.* JERZY *doubles up.* DUSTY *is about to punch him again.)*

DUSTY: How do you like that, you little shit? Huh, huh, how do you...

(Now ANNA LEE *jumps on his back and begins to pull his hair.* DUSTY *screams in pain.)*

ANNA LEE: Let him alone! Let my boy friend alone!

*(*LITTLE J *now tries to pull* ANNA LEE *off of* DUSTY'S *back.)*

LITTLE J: Anna Lee, please! Come on, come on! Let's cool it, come on, let's just....

*(*ANNA LEE *falls off* DUSTY'S *back.)*

DUSTY: *(To* ANNA LEE*)* You bitch! I oughtta punch you in the mouth!

(Now JERZY *tackles* DUSTY. *The two of them start rolling around on the ground, grappling, punching, cursing.)*

JERZY: I'll kill you! Hurt my girl friend! I'll spill your fascist blood!

(Now JAMES enters.)

JAMES: Damnit! What's going on here? I leave you alone for ten minutes and…geez. Come on, Little J., give me a hand!

(JAMES and LITTLE J start pulling JERZY and DUSTY off each other. Finally they get them separated.)

DUSTY: I'm not going to work on this stupid play anymore! Look what she did to my damned arm! *(There's a nasty scratch on his arm.)* And him! *(Pointing to JERZY)* He's out of his goddamned mind! A maniac who doesn't know the difference between acting and reality! You should see him backstage, throwing me around and screaming: *(Doing JERZY's accent)* I kill you fucking fascist freak! For all your ugly fascist crimes you die!

JERZY: What I am executing is a lesson in acting! Is acting no longer permissible in the theater? Is this not still a free country for acting? I humbly besiege you to correct me if I am wrong!

JAMES: Ahh, shut up, Jerzy! Okay! Just shut up!

(ANNA LEE starts to cry.)

DUSTY: And what's this damned stupid—what do you call it—theater piece, about anyway? Nothing but hating America, and complaining about Vietnam, is all I can see!

LITTLE J: Hey, it's more subtle than that, Dusty. Give it a chance.

(ANNA LEE is sobbing hysterically now. JERZY is bending over her, trying to soothe her.)

JAMES: Quiet down, Anna Lee! Don't you realize how goddamned unprofessional this all is?

(ANNA LEE's sobs grow louder.)

JAMES: Jerzy, will you get her the hell out of here! And make it fast!

(JERZY *puts his arm around* ANNA LEE *and starts to walk her out of the room. Now* DUSTY *starts to leave.*)

JAMES: Wait a minute, Dusty, I want to talk to you.

(DUSTY *stops.*)

JAMES: This will never happen again, I swear. I'll keep them in line.

DUSTY: I can live with them, and even with this damned play that I don't like; but the big question is, what the hell am I really learning about acting? And how is it going to help my career?

JAMES: You're learning how to die, Dusty.

DUSTY: Wow, that's just great.

JAMES: Pentheus, is Dionysus' surrogate. He has to be sacrificed in the spring, so that the grapes that are holy to the god, symbolic of his life, can grow again; in other words, in order for Dionysus to be reborn, Pentheus must die. What we're doing here, Dusty, is learning something about death and rebirth.

DUSTY: Great, that's really great. Really fucking cool, if you're some kind of anthropologist. But the truth is, all this religious crap leaves me cold. (*He exits.*)

JAMES: I'm afraid that this piece is falling apart, Little J, and I'm just not coming up with the right answers.

LITTLE J: No, man. You're giving. You really are. We're on the verge of doing something really important, doing something great, because…

(*Suddenly* LITTLE J *grabs hold of* JAMES *and fiercely embraces him.*)

LITTLE J: Because guys like us do what we have to do! What our heart tells us to do! Isn't that right, fucking

Ranger? You and I are like that! We really are! *(He lets go of him.)*

JAMES: Yeah, I guess we are, Little J. In some strange way.

(Darkness. We hear Le Sacre du Printemps *playing in the background.)*

(JAMES and REGINE are in their bedroom. JAMES has just entered the room. REGINE is looking out the window, her back to him. Now he walks over to her and puts his hand on her shoulder. Her body visibly recoils.)

JAMES: Why did you do that?

REGINE: What?

JAMES: Jump like that.

REGINE: Well, you frightened me. Touched me.

JAMES: Touched you? You mean me touching you automatically frightens you?

REGINE: I wasn't expecting it.

JAMES: Next time I'll phone ahead.

(REGINE looks at JAMES, a slightly sarcastic smile on her face.)

REGINE: You do that.

JAMES: Listen, Regine, there's something that I've been meaning to ask you for a long time now.

REGINE: Oh. And what is that?

JAMES: I've always wanted you to explain your unhappiness to me. The true nature of it. Could you do that for me, Regine? Explain your unhappiness to me.

REGINE: *(Blinking at him, as if a voice a thousand miles away was speaking to her.)* But if I did, it would be too precise, and nobody would be able to stand if.

Especially you, James. And then what would we do? I
mean, how would we be able to survive?

JAMES: I don't know, Regine. But I think you're right
about trying to survive. Because what else do we have
left?

(REGINE *smiles strangely at* JAMES.)

(Darkness. The lights come back up. JAMES *is alone on stage,
in the same position as we last saw him. The train whistle
is heard in the background; maybe a faint glow of red. Now,
over the sound system, we begin to hear bits and pieces of
the fight* SANDY *and* JAMES *had concerning his play. As
the fight grows,* JAMES *starts to move, going on some secret
journey, following a broken path across the stage.)*

SANDY: And those poor stupid kids—they way you
manipulate them! I find it totally offensive; disgusting,
really, what you do... Talk about fascism, talk about
dictators, you take the damned...

JAMES: That's not true! I don't manipulate them. It's a
collaboration, it's....

SANDY: Semi-ignorant kids who know next to nothing
about politics, about their country or its history,
nothing about the real meaning of the war! Not to
mention life!

JAMES: Students, you mean; not kids! Students who
know enough to know that they don't want to get
themselves killed! Or to kill anyone else either!

SANDY: FRAGMENTS OF THE MOTHER! That bloody
abortion thrown on the stage! Actors climbing all
over the place, screaming, incoherent maniacs, violent
lunatics. Just meaningless crap!

JAMES: What the hell do you know? What the hell have
you ever accomplished that makes you so goddamned
knowledgeable, that makes you so damned...

SANDY: And the state pays you for doing things like that? Unbelievable! Some people think that you should be shot, you know.

JAMES: Good. I want people to have a reaction.

SANDY: Oh, they will! They really will. Just wait till you see all the wonderful reactions people start having when they read the letter I'm writing, explaining not only how you waste their damned money but also how you undermine the very values that....

JAMES: What people? What people are you talking about?

SANDY: People in the university system, people in the state government, that's who!

JAMES: That's a wonderful idea! I'm amazed that you thought it up all by yourself.

SANDY: You bastard! You'll see, you really will!

(The sound abruptly stops. At the back of the stage we are able to see the faintly luminescent outline of a large American flag. JAMES *continues walking. He is now working his way through the darkness, a hubbub of sounds and possibly images: the voices of students, shouts, murmurs, whispers, etc.; trucks moving about at a distance, tanks possibly? people marching in a peace march, soldiers? —rock 'n roll, cars traveling down the highway, the sound of a train and its ever present whistle. Gradually his mind clears. He now finds himself at a gathering, a party at a farm just outside of town. Somewhere along the line, he realizes, that without really knowing it, he has been looking for* SANDY. *Suddenly he sees her, almost like an apparition, a drink in her hand, sitting on a bench, under a large oak tree. The moon hangs precariously overhead. Everything is silent now as he stares at her; the rest of the party has suddenly disappeared.)*

JAMES: Well, look who's here, sitting under the old apple tree.

SANDY: *(Surprised)* Oh! Have you come to continue our fight?

JAMES: That was weeks ago.

SANDY: But you haven't forgotten, have you?

JAMES: Not really. But somehow I think it's just too beautiful a night to ruin with an argument.

SANDY: Far too. *(Pause)* So you want to call a temporary truce or something?

JAMES: Sure. Why not?

SANDY: But most of the things I said, I can't take back, because they're true, you know.

JAMES: Who's asking you to?

(Music is heard in the background.)

SANDY: *(She stares intently at him for a few moments.)* You see, I've been thinking, there's something that I want to say to you. I mean, you might find this hard to believe, but I'd like to talk to you about something, well, sensitive. And this may be my only opportunity—but if you don't want to, if I'm really annoying you, just tell me to get lost and I'll understand.

JAMES: Go ahead. What do you want to talk about?

SANDY: Something bothers me, you see, something seems to be missing from my life. And I don't know how to get to it, because oddly enough, I don't even know what it is. *(She laughs a little.)* I mean, I'm not a talented person or anything. Sure, I've tried acting, even directing, but it was all too amateurish and pathetic to take seriously. I came here simply because I thought it would be nice to get a Masters, maybe teach high school. But still, I'm filled with all this "stuff," this really volatile stuff, that I don't know what to do with.

JAMES: Go on.

SANDY: You see, it only took me a month or so to realize that this place was a big mistake. The only course I really liked was Shakespeare. Everything else was a terrible bore. So I decided to leave; until, as fate would have it, I saw your play.

JAMES: And you found yourself totally captivated.

SANDY: Yes! By how much I hated it! But somehow I also felt—and this is the weird part—totally alive! Like I was suddenly on some kind of sacred mission or something! So I stayed up half the night, writing down everything that I loved and hated about America; and things about myself, too, that I had never thought about before. And by morning my suspicions were confirmed.

JAMES: What suspicions?

SANDY: Ahh, well, and this is not easy to say; but, I felt, that it would be possible to communicate with you, in some strange kind of way—if I could only get over my anger towards you. Which I knew wouldn't be such an easy thing to do.

(JAMES *laughs*.)

SANDY: I'm not saying that I started liking you as a person, or anything like that. I'm just talking about communication.

JAMES: You can say whatever you want to me.

SANDY: *(A slight pause here)* Alright, I will. Because I think I have to say whatever it is, whatever comes out. No censorship. Otherwise it would be worthless.

JAMES: Go right ahead.

SANDY: So hold on to your hat. *(A beat, and then…)* I think about you all the time, it seems. Days and days. I just keep thinking of you. What are these thoughts

really? It's hard to say. They'll probably go away,
sooner or later. Don't you think? I'm sure they will.
Thoughts have a tendency to do that, run themselves
down, disappear. I'm hoping that will be the case; but
in the meantime, I can't stop them having their way
with me, the way they're doing now. I just can't get rid
of them.

(JAMES *wants to say something, but can't find the words.*)

SANDY: But I will, I'm sure. With a little luck.

(The lights go to dark and then come back up. SANDY *and*
JAMES *have danced and had a few drinks together, and are
now back under the tree. Moonlight, the grass glistening, the
sound of insects.)*

SANDY: But I hate myself, sometimes, for wanting, you
know, certain things, as much as I do.

JAMES: Why?

SANDY: Because so often they're the wrong things.

JAMES: So what. We want all kinds of things. God
knows what we want?

SANDY: I'm selfish, you see; it's a family trait. I'm
trying to warn you. Underneath it all, it could be that
I'm really not a very nice, idealistic person at all. When
you get down to it, I may be nothing but a thief and a
liar and a whore. So don't be taken in by my sincerity.
Because I'm certainly not.

(JAMES *starts to laugh.)*

SANDY: It's not funny. I had this aunt, a terrible and
beautiful aunt. One day, when I was about thirteen,
she took me out in her garden, and sat me down on
a bench and said to me: "Sandra, most importantly,
don't let them know who you really are, or how much
you know, or what you really do. Because secrets are
power, Sandra, especially for Southern women."

JAMES: I guess things really are different down there.

SANDY: Sure, because someday, who knows, you might want to take yourself a nice looking black lover, or maybe even some nasty radical professor for fun.

JAMES: *(Without realizing what he is saying.)* I'm not really a professor just... *(Suddenly embarrassed, he turns away from her.)*

SANDY: I'm sorry. I should leave you alone, stop bothering you. Stop teasing you like this.

(SANDY starts to leave. JAMES grabs her hand.)

SANDY: Being that we're hated enemies and all. Heated enemies, and all.

(JAMES holds SANDY's hand for a second or two longer and then lets it go.)

JAMES: What brought you up here, anyway? Why did you pick this school, out of all the schools in America?

SANDY: Blame Professor Harris. He's a close friend of my uncle, the general. They were in the war together. I've known him since I was a child. He was always begging me to call him Uncle Harry, but I never would.

JAMES: How come?

SANDY: Because there always seemed something just a little bit weird lurking behind those eyes of his.

JAMES: So Harry Harris was the one who got you to come here! Unbelievable!

(The sound of the music is cranked up. Now we see the figure of the SPEAKER, in faint outline, before the American flag.)

SPEAKER: Are we going to let them rule us?

CROWD: *(Screaming)* Noooooo.

SPEAKER: Let them tell us who we are, let them tell us what not to do, let them keep us from saying FUCK YOU TO YOUR DEATH TRIP AMERIKA?!

CROWD: *(Screaming)* Nooooooo.

SPEAKER: So what are we going to do about it?

CROWD: Overthrow the status quo!
Support those who won't go!
Overthrow, overthrow, overthrow!
Support those who won't go!

(The flag seems to be glowing.)

SANDY: Sometimes it seems people just want to bang into each other, real hard with their bodies. Slam into each other. Maybe for all the wrong reasons.

JAMES: Yeah. For power.

SANDY: Or just to hurt themselves, or perhaps the other.

JAMES: Or for pleasure, maybe.

SANDY: Do you think these people, should be shot, should be punished? I used to think so, not too long ago.

JAMES: It's the American way: do what you want, do it all, and think about it tomorrow.

SANDY: You want to see if you can win. Like politics. Come out on top. Like our political leaders. Or on the other hand, maybe you'll lose. End up with your face in the dirt. End up being destroyed.

JAMES: But I look into your eyes, and I think not—that it's not just about winning and losing. That there's something else going on.

SANDY: Don't look into my eyes. *(But she doesn't turn away.)*

(The outline of the American flag seems to grow brighter, maybe even larger.)

JAMES: The flag flying overhead. Overshadowing us. Enfolding us. Freight trains hauling a thousand cars, burning red across the prairies. Burning through our dreams.

SANDY: Getting drunk and lonely in the midst of America; this great campus hanging by a thread from the stars, swaying above the fires. This great mind, swaying above the fires. Containing thousands and thousands...lonely brilliant minds, heading straight towards one another, streaming towards...like comets; sometimes for all the wrong reasons. Abstract, remote, but still wanting, aching. Enemies, perhaps, but still bright with desire. Like God, aching eternally, like God. Though He knows how imperfect it all is, that it will never give Him what He really desires. Still He cannot, will not turn away. *(She laughs a little.)* Oh, I've romanticized it, I'm afraid; much too much. Haven't I? Even dragged God into it.

SPEAKER: Are we going to let them rule us?

CROWD: *(Screaming)* Noooooo.

SPEAKER: Let them tell us who we are, let them tell us what not to do, let them keep us from saying FUCK YOU TO YOUR DEATH TRIP AMERIKA?!

CROWD: *(Screaming)* Nooooooo.

SPEAKER: So what are going to do about it?

CROWD: Overthrow the status quo!
Overthrow, overthrow, overthrow!

(The flag bursts into flames. JAMES and SANDY cry out. Their bodies slam into each other. They grab hold of each other tightly. Now, everything seems to be on fire, even their bodies, burning as they sink to the ground. The shriek of the red train. Darkness)

(SANDY and JAMES are in a barn, lying down in the hay, where they have made love. Early morning light penetrates the scene; the sound of animals.)

SANDY: I like the smell. In fact, I love it. It smells like the south, the deep shit of it. *(She laughs.)* I'll bet they don't have many barns left in New York City, do they? *(She gets to her feet, moving away from him a bit, going into the shadows, exploring.)*

JAMES: No. But they should. They certainly can come in handy. *(Suddenly seeing that she is not there next to him)* Sandy?

SANDY: What? I'm just exploring. *(She starts walking into the darkness.)*

JAMES: *(Suddenly panicking)* No! I've got to hold you! I need to hold you! C'mere, so's that I can.... Just so I can...protect you, Sandy! *(Crying out)* Sandy, please!

(Suddenly someone seems to grab hold of her. She tries to fight, cry out, but her voice is cut off, as she is dragged struggling into the darkness.)

JAMES: Sandy, Sandy! Noooo! *(But he is trapped in his nightmare; he can't move, can't help, or reach her, only able to cry out.)* Sandy, pleassseeee!

(Darkness)

(JAMES is in STONES' office. STONES has just told him to sit down, but JAMES stares blankly at him, as if he didn't know who he was or what he was saying to him.)

STONES: I told you to sit the fuck down. Are you deaf or something?

(Now JAMES's mind begins to clear.)

JAMES: What did you say?

STONES: For you to sit the fuck down, is what I just said.

JAMES: *(He sits down.)* I thought that there was no cursing allowed during a murder investigation?

STONES: The rules have suddenly changed.

JAMES: Oh, have they?

STONES: Yes, they have.

JAMES: And what brought that about?

STONES: I've become *you*, you see.

JAMES: What?

STONES: *You*, I've become *you*. A part of you anyway, a part of me anyway. In order to save you.

(At this point JAMES *notices that* STONES *now looks something like him—clothes, hairdo, mannerisms, etc.)*

JAMES: That's quite a trick.

STONES: Yes, I've become my enemy. Gone into the jungle and become one with the man I hunt. And at quite a cost to myself, I might say.

JAMES: I'm afraid that you're hallucinating on this one, Stones. Way out there without a map or a compass this time, Stones.

STONES: Don't worry. Sooner or later you'll learn the truth, professor.

JAMES: And what truth is that, Stones?

STONES: That at rock bottom we're the same. No difference at all, between us.

JAMES: But that's not true, detective.

STONES: Oh, but I'm afraid it is. I'm a killer, and you're a murderer.

JAMES: Then if we're equal, why not let me go free? Like you.

STONES: Because the law says I must hunt you.

JAMES: And what about you? Who hunts you, detective?

STONES: That's something I take care of myself.

JAMES: No! You hunt others! That's who you hunt!

(Suddenly STONES *grabs* JAMES' *hand. A strange energy passes into* JAMES, *disorientating him.* JAMES *desperately tries to free his hand from* STONES' *grasp but is unable to.)*

STONES: You're a strong man, professor. Come on now, arm wrestle me. Go ahead. Just for fun. Try your strength against mine.

*(*STONES *places* JAMES' *hand in the arm wrestling position.)*

JAMES: Okay, okay. I will.

(They begin to struggle fiercely. After a few seconds JAMES *manages to put* STONES' *arm down.)*

STONES: Yes, you're a very strong man, brother! You can do anything you want!

JAMES: No. You let me win! *(He pulls away from* STONES, *and gets to his feet.)* I have to go home now.

*(*JAMES *tries to find the door, but he can't find it—desperate, he crashes into the wall, then begins pounding it with his fists, as if trying to break through.* STONES *watches him for a few moments.)*

STONES: You lied to me.

JAMES: What?

STONES: You had an affair with Sandra, didn't you?

JAMES: No.

STONES: A letter came to us, an anonymous letter, filled with telling details.

JAMES: Whoever wrote it is the liar.

STONES: Your marriage is not predominately a happy one. Is it?

JAMES: You have no right to touch my marriage!

STONES: I have the right to touch anything I want. *(He starts walking towards* JAMES.) *And now I'm going to

take you and put you in a jail cell, and lock the door on
you. And there you'll stay, until you find the strength
to speak the truth and save your Almighty soul.

(JAMES *is panicked, but his mind gradually comes back to
him.*)

JAMES: Listen. You're right. I did lie to you.

STONES: Go on.

JAMES: I was afraid to tell you the truth.

STONES: What truth, exactly?

JAMES: How much I hated her, how much I despised
and loathed Sandra Townsend. Because I was afraid
that it would be used against me.

(STONES *just stares at* JAMES.)

JAMES: I hated her and her whole right wing ruling
class family! Everybody knew that. Everybody knew
how I felt. I could barely stand being in the same room
with that right wing bitch! How many kids sacrificed
for her families' goddamned history and honor!?! Ha!
And you think that I could actually have had an affair
with her? Put my hands on her in some intimate way?
(*He starts to laugh.*) So let's talk straight, brother, man
to man. Because you're right, we really are brothers
down deep, aren't we? The only difference being, you
kill on the field of battle, and I kill in my heart. You
see, I so intensively loathed that right wing whore, that
I wouldn't have fucked her with Nixon's dick! And
I'll tell you something even worse—something that
you might want to hurt me with later—but I wasn't
particularly sorry to see her go either. Not at all! (*He
laughs, then stops.*) In the context of reality, I thought it
was a good thing somebody killed her.

STONES: Get the hell out of here.

JAMES: Yeah, sure, okay. But aren't we even going
to have a little prayer together? I was really looking
forward to a little midday prayer, brother.

(STONES *puts his hand on his gun.*)

JAMES: You want to shoot me, detective? Then go
ahead. Do yourself a favor. Do us both a fucking favor!
(*He turns his back on* STONES *and exits.*)

(*Darkness. The lights come back up. Night.* JAMES *is outside
now in a field. The sky whirling wildly above him*)

JAMES: Sandy! Oh, Sandy! Where are you? (*Suddenly,
violently, crying out...*) Sandy! What have I done?

(*The sound of the red train, not too far away, a thousand
cars, going a hundred miles an hour, heading towards him.
Bearing down on him. Darkness*)

(*It is late at night.* JAMES *is sitting at his desk in his office,
writing furiously in a notebook. We hear Stravinsky's* Le
Sacre du Printemps, *playing on a scratchy old record.
After a few moments* HARRIS *appears at the half open door
and watches* JAMES *writing; now he steps back and knocks
on the door.* JAMES *looks up. The music stops abruptly.*)

HARRIS: James! How are you? I was prowling about,
and saw that your light was on, so I thought that I'd
drop by and...

JAMES: I'm sorry, Harry, but I was just on my way
home, you see, so...

(*Before* JAMES *can finish,* HARRIS *is inside and sitting at his
desk. He is quite drunk, and carrying his ubiquitous coffee
cup.* JAMES *puts the notebook in his desk.*)

HARRIS: Let me buy you a drink, James. It would give
me great pleasure.

JAMES: No thanks, Harry. I've got other things on my
mind.

HARRIS: Oh, come on. Loosen up, hippie! *(He laughs then pulls a pint bottle out of jacket, grabs a cup off of* JAMES's *desk and pours some whiskey in it, then gives it to* JAMES.*)* Here's to life. And to that crazy old Gent who started us off on this cockeyed planet of His.

*(*HARRIS *and* JAMES *drink.)*

HARRIS: Mister Shit-for-brains, I like to call Him. *(He laughs.)*

JAMES: *(Drinking up)* Well, Harry, thanks for the drink, but now... *(He starts to get up.)*

HARRIS: *(Coldly)* Sit down.

JAMES: What, Harry?

HARRIS: *(Changing his tone)* Oh, just for a minute or two. I mean, how often do I get to have a first rate intellectual conversation with a gifted equal?

JAMES: I'm not sure. How often?

HARRIS: Not very often. *(Pulls out a book and puts it on the desk with some emphasis.)* Christopher Marlowe! Kit Marlowe, I like to call him. Some people called him Marley. You like him, James, his writing?

JAMES: He was a good writer.

HARRIS: Good writer?!? Far far more than that, James! What language, what a mind! And certainly not afraid of the dark side of the street. Some say he was a faggot. Probably was. But I don't hold that against him. Some called him Marley. A man who was as good with a sword as he was with a pen. Killed a man in a duel. Eventually was murdered himself. Stabbed in the eye, James, that eye that saw so much, beauty. I drink to your memory, Kit, Kit Marlowe, ink squitterer, par excellence. *(He drinks.)*

JAMES: Well, Harry, it's been a pleasure, but...

HARRIS: If I were an Elizabethan, I'd call you out, James.

JAMES: What?

HARRIS: I'd call you out, challenge you to a duel, I'm saying.

JAMES: Why would you do that, Harry?

HARRIS: Because I would be hoping to kill you, that's why.

JAMES: *(Starting to leave)* Let's just call it a night, alright, Harry? Let's just call it quits, this intellectual discussion among equals that we're having.

HARRIS: *(Laughing)* Wait, wait, wait. Hey, hey, hold on, young guy. The problem is, James, that I lost my train of thought. Lost our mutual fantasy. A few moments ago, we were back in the reign of Virgina Regina, or was it Vagina Regina? *(He laughs.)* What the hell! I'm talking about the Queen! A grand grand lady. And there we were, chatting about Kit Marlowe. Just the two of us, deep in our muddy boots, rapiers at our sides. Drunk to the fucking gizzard!

JAMES: You know, Harry. I don't give a damn about any of it! None of it, Harry!

HARRIS: You don't give a damn about any of it? The mud and the glory, the language and the splendor that was Elizabethan fucking England! And you call yourself a man of the theater?

JAMES: And I don't give a damn about you either, Harry, or what you're saying.

HARRIS: Well, let me tell you, I take that remark as an insult, not only to myself, but also to Kit Marlowe; and thus, I call you out, face to face, man to man, James. Your choice of weapons, of course. Steel or pistol. Or whatever else you might feel comfortable with.

JAMES: I won't fight you.

HARRIS: Why's that, because you're a pathetic little, draft-dodger, who's too afraid to step into the ring with a decorated war hero?

JAMES: Haven't we had enough killing, Harry?

HARRIS: It's blood for blood now, James. Blood for blood.

JAMES: What are you saying, Harry?

HARRIS: You know exactly what I'm saying, James. Exactly what I'm talking about.

(HARRIS *moves towards* JAMES, *who begins to back away from him.*)

JAMES: Go home, Harry. Give it up and go the hell home!

HARRIS: Not until I run over you, shitbird!

(HARRIS *rushes at him.* JAMES *moves out of his way.*)

HARRIS: That's right, run, run! *(Laughing)* You don't stand a chance, James! Because I'm a decorated war hero! Wounded twice on a Jap island! Look at this! *(He pulls his coat off and throws it in the corner. Now he rips open his shirt.)* Look, you little shitbird! Look at these scars! There's the proof, there's… *(He peers at his body, looking for the scars, but is unable to see them.)* Where the hell are they? What happened to my scars? They were there this morning, I swear! Perhaps I'm too drunk to see them? Perhaps I wasn't fighting the Japs when they shot me that time but instead was running away from them. Who the hell knows for sure? Because most people are dead these days! Including those we love! And now I want my satisfaction! Ripeness is all! *(He begins moving towards* JAMES, *throwing punches as he comes.)* Fight me! Come on! Think I'm some WASP faggot, can't take a punch! I'll show you what I can take. Come oooonnnn! (*Suddenly, wildly, he begins punching himself in the face.*) Come ooonnnnnn! Come on, come on, come on! Hit me! Hit me! You muck-faced bunch of moronical, shit eating baboons! I'll show you all!

JAMES: Stop it, Harry! You're out of your damned mind!

(JAMES *tries to stop him, but by the time he does* HARRIS's *face is streaming with blood.*)

JAMES: Just look at you, Harry! Look what you did to yourself!

(HARRIS *grins, then collapses in a chair, laughing a bit.*)

JAMES: Here, take my handkerchief.

(JAMES *hands* HARRIS *his handkerchief. Now* HARRIS *begins to pat his face, whimpering piteously at the same time.*)

HARRIS: Look what you did to me, James.

JAMES: I never touched you, Harry.

HARRIS: You beat me senseless. What the fuck for?

JAMES: That's a lie!

HARRIS: Who'd believe you? A man being investigated for murder! (*He laughs.*) Do you deny it? What you did? You can't fool me or Detective Stones. Your time's running out, James. Soon the truth will be told. And you'll have to pay dearly!

JAMES: What are you saying, Harry?

HARRIS: That I'm not afraid to speak the truth, the truth that has not yet been spoken!

JAMES: You sent that anonymous letter, didn't you?

HARRIS: Anonymous! Why, I've never had an anonymous a day in my life!

JAMES: So what's this truth that you're about to speak, Harry?

HARRIS: She came to me. She told me everything.

JAMES: Who? Sandy?

HARRIS: Yes. Sandra Townsend came to me. Does that surprise you?

JAMES: Yes, it does. And what did she say to you?

HARRIS: None of your business, asswipe.

(JAMES *cries out, then grabbing* HARRIS *by the shirt, pulls back his fist as if to hit him.*)

HARRIS: Don't hit me!

JAMES: I will hit you! I'll kill you! What did she say to you?

HARRIS: She said that the two of you had an affair! *(He begins to sob.)* It's disgusting! It really is. *(Seeing her in his mind's eye)* Sandra, Sandra, what are you saying to me? I can't believe it!

JAMES: Pull yourself together, Harry.

HARRIS: The two of you! I knew her since she was this high. She came to me because she was distraught, terribly upset. I never saw her like that before. Shocking, shocking.

JAMES: What did she say to you, Harry?

HARRIS: She said, that you used her and then dumped her; had your pleasure and then crawled back to your wife!

(JAMES *doesn't answer.*)

HARRIS: You bastard, where did you get the power to do that?

JAMES: I didn't mean to hurt her.

HARRIS: I wanted so much, to comfort her, to touch her. *(He is sobbing profusely now.)* I said, Sandra, let me comfort you, let me touch you. Let me run my hands up your legs, darling Sandra. Just to feel your lovely legs, is all I want. To give you some pleasure is all I desire.

JAMES: Did she let you, Harry?

HARRIS: Yes, so I slipped my hands under her dress, and... *(There is an ecstatic look in his eyes, as he mimes running his hands under dress.)* Just her legs, just her legs. It was enough. Her beautiful silky legs.

JAMES: You were in love with her, weren't you, Harry?

HARRIS: What? Yes. Ever since she was a child. I adored her.

JAMES: She took pity on you, Harry. That's what she did. *(He starts to leave, but then stops.)* But you wouldn't hurt her, would you, Harry? *(He stops and stares at him.)* Ever hurt her. Would you, Harry?

HARRIS: Anybody but her. Anybody but her, James. Unlike you.

(JAMES starts walking off into the darkness.)

JAMES: Sandy. Sandy where are you? Sandy!

(Darkness)

(JAMES has just entered the old barn where he and SANDY had made love. It is dark inside. He looks around trying to find her. Now we hear her voice.)

SANDY: Up there! Look! Bats hunting in the barn-light!

JAMES: *(Seeing her)* Oh, Sandy!

SANDY: I'll bet you don't see that very often in New York.

(JAMES rushes to SANDY. They embrace, then kiss.)

JAMES: God, you're beautiful, Sandy!

SANDY: No, I'm not. I'm past my prime. My looks are already beginning to fade.

JAMES: Really? No!

SANDY: Sure, look. *(She holds up her face.)*

JAMES: *(Examining her)* Wellll, there and there, a little bit. But basically I think you're wrong. You'll be alright, for another six months or so, at least.

SANDY: Thanks. *(She growls at him.)*

(Suddenly we hear an explosion of sharp cries, whistles, drumming, then DUSTY, as Pentheus, comes racing across the stage, looking for a place to hide. Now ANNA LEE, JERZY and LITTLE J, come rushing on, looking for him. The whole effect is like a vivid dream, a surreal hallucination cutting into JAMES and SANDY's reality.)

JAMES: *(Pointing out where DUSTY is hiding)* He's there! He's over there!

SANDY: Don't tell them!

JAMES: *(Pointing out where DUSTY is hiding)* He's there! He's over there!

SANDY: Don't tell them!

(As they go to the place that JAMES has just pointed out, DUSTY comes running out of another spot.)

JAMES: No, no! He's here now! He's right here! *(Pointing into the shadows nearby)*

SANDY: Let him escape this time!

(The CHORUS rushes out, hot on DUSTY's trail. Out of sight, in the darkness, they fall upon him, and then begin to tear him apart. DUSTY's cries are quite terrible to hear.)

JAMES: Geez, he's really acting that now. He's really into it. Good for you, Dusty!

(After a few moments the chorus comes rushing out, jubilant, and splattered with blood. The men are each holding

an arm or a leg, ANNA LEE, *a human head, triumphantly in the air.)*

JAMES: She thinks that it's the head of a mountain lion. But it's her own son.

SANDY: Lovely, really lovely. *(She turns away.)*

CHORUS: Freedom! Freedom to worship Dionysus! Freedom for those who dare follow the god! Freedom, freedom, freedom! For those who dare pay the price! Freedom!

(They dance wildly about, then disappear into the darkness.)

SANDY: I hate this rotten, blood-soaked play!

JAMES: The god demanded his death.

SANDY: What good is a god like that, a murdering god like that?

JAMES: I could say the same about the god you worship, Ares the god of war.

SANDY: You really think that's the god I worship, some killing god, some worthless, murderous god like that?

JAMES: Yeah, in one way or another, I'm afraid I do.

SANDY: Then you can go to hell!

JAMES: And you to the god you love so much! Ares the flesh eater! Standing in the muck in his blood soaked jungle boots, licking his filthy chops!

SANDY: You sonofabitch! *(She goes towards him, raising her hand as if to hit him, then pulls back.)* No! I won't hit you, I won't touch you, I won't do anything with you. You can just go to hell! Coward, traitor! *(She begins to sob.)*

JAMES: Listen, Sandy, I'm sorry.

SANDY: No, you're not. Not at all. In your mind it's me, people like me who are behind it all, the war, the carnage—isn't that true?

JAMES: No, it's not true. What I really want is the body of America to be healed, to come together, as it should be. And the same for us, Sandy. I want us to come together too, and stay together. Forever, Sandy. Because that's what should be.

SANDY: No. I don't believe you. Sometimes I think that you really hate me, that you'd like to kill me, or something.

JAMES: (*Going towards her.*) No, Sandy, that's not true. (*He touches her. She recoils.*) I want you, Sandy.

SANDY: Who cares what you want! Go back to your family, your wife.(*She takes out a tissue and begins to dab her eyes and blow her nose.*) You haven't even left her, so what's the big deal? (*Angry now*) A lot of the times I don't feel so great about you either. To hell with you! You don't know what you're like. Sometimes you actually make me sick. (*She sits down on a bale of hay and lights up a cigarette.*)

JAMES: I thought that you'd quit smoking.

SANDY: I'm suffering a relapse.

JAMES: Be careful, Sandy, you might set the place on fire.

SANDY: Who cares? Everything's burning up anyway. People would hardly notice.

(*We hear the sound of the animals.*)

JAMES: The animals wouldn't much like it. In fact, I think they're starting to complain already.

SANDY: Somehow I forgot what I wanted from you in the first place, what I was after. But now it doesn't matter. Who cares? (*She exhales smoke.*) Now I'm completely on my own.

JAMES: Have patience with me, Sandy, have patience.

SANDY: *(Now she carefully puts out her cigarette.)* Listen, let me tell you a little story. You see, I have this girl cousin, a favorite cousin, exactly a year and a half older than me—actually more like a sister than a cousin, we were so close. And one day she decides to get a degree in journalism, up north in your territory at Columbia University. And when she finishes her work she comes back home and gets a job at the local paper. Well, it turns out that General William Childs Westmoreland is on vacation from the war, and staying with friends in the area; and my cousin also hears that every day he plays tennis in this country club, where she is also a member. And it should be noted, that General William Childs Westmoreland, hates and despises interviews. But this does not deter my intrepid girl cousin, who seeks the General out at the country club, and after enveloping him in a flirtatious cloud of rosy southern banter, actually wangles an interview with him. Well, the interview comes off as scheduled, and is printed in the Sunday edition of our local paper. And guess what my cousin was able to accomplish in her interview? Why, quite simply and economically, just by twisting a few of his words, here and there, and leaving out a fact or two, there and here, and by stressing her own very strong point of view, she was able to make General William Childs Westmoreland look like an inept, cold blooded killer, a heartless destroyer of his own men! *(Pause)* And do you know what General Westmoreland said, when he read her words?

JAMES: No. But I think I can guess.

SANDY: If I ever get my hands on her, I'll kill her! I swear, I'll strangle that miserable bitch!

JAMES: Why did she write it, Sandy?

SANDY: Why? Because she had a favorite cousin of her own, a boy cousin, who went to West Point, and was killed in Vietnam. And she always blamed the General for his death, said that Westmoreland murdered her cousin. *(Pause)* I hit her in the face, you know. It was at a party, a garden party. She stood up, came right up to me like always, smiling, "Sandy, how nice to see you..." And she never expected, thought, what I might do to her—hit her so hard, this cousin, hurt my hand, this cousin that I loved more than my own sister.

JAMES: *(He goes to her, taking her hand...)* Sandy, listen, no more. We'll have our own moratorium, the two of us, we won't talk about the war anymore. We'll be totally apolitical. *(He kisses her hand.)*

SANDY: I don't think it's possible.

JAMES: Sure, it's possible. And you were right about the play: no more violence, we don't need any more violence now. It's no longer the time for it.

SANDY: But what can you do without violence? It's your theatrical specialty.

JAMES: Well, I've got this idea to make a new piece, a piece based on Whitman's poetry, stressing healing, spirituality, our erotic natures, you know, cool stuff like that.

SANDY: He was originally from the New York area, wasn't he?

JAMES: Whitman? Yes, he was. But try and ignore that piece of information, Sandy, and just concentrate on his spirit.

SANDY: A supporter of the war of northern aggression, I suppose.

JAMES: More of a supporter of the human condition. Listen to these lines:
Battles, the horrors of fratricidal war, the fever of
     doubtful news, the fitful events;
These come to me days and nights and go from me

again,
But they are not the Me myself.
I am the poet of the Body and I am the poet of the Soul,
The pleasures of heaven are with me and the pains of
    hell are with me.
I am the poet of the woman the same as the man,
And I say it is as great to be a woman as to be a man,
And I say there is nothing greater than the mother of
    men.

SANDY: Hey, that's neat. And also totally true.

JAMES: Smile O voluptuous cool-breath'd earth!
Earth of the slumbering and liquid trees!
Rich apple-blossom'd earth!
Smile, for your lover comes.

Prodigal, you have given me love—therefore I to you
give love!
O unspeakable passionate love.

SANDY: Oh, that's nice. That's really nice.

JAMES: You sea!

SANDY: *(Looking straight at him)* Yes?

JAMES: I resign myself to you—I guess what you mean,
I believe you refuse to go back without feeling of me.
We must have a turn together, I undress,
Hurry me out of sight of the land,
Cushion me soft, rock me in billowy drowse,
Dash me with amorous wet, I can repay you.

SANDY: Can you?

JAMES: I can repay you. I will repay you.

(JAMES and SANDY embrace. Now they kiss.)

JAMES: I will, Sandy. I swear, I will, I will, I will repay
you.

END OF ACT TWO

ACT THREE

(The lights come up on a somewhat abstract rendering of an old fashioned, residential street in a midwestern town. It is lined with large three story houses and ancient elm trees. Suddenly there is a large explosion, a flash of fire, and the sound of a man screaming. Darkness)

(JAMES' office at the university. ANNA LEE, JERZY and LITTLE J have just entered.)

JAMES: So tell me, what the hell happened?

JERZY: Bombers! We've got bombers in town!

LITTLE J: I saw it! It was unbelievable! There I was, walking down Jackson Street. It was about ten in the morning. A beautiful sunshiny day. I'm having, what you might call: a God's alive and working hard in the midwest, kind of experience. The paper boy's riding along on his bike, flipping his newspapers onto porches. His little dog running along behind him.

ANNA LEE: *I* used to be a paper girl when I was twelve. I was great at it. I won a major award for courtesy.

LITTLE J: Then all of a sudden—I mean, right behind me!—BAM! There's this huge explosion! And a big chunk of the top floor of this house is blown out onto the street. Scared the living hell out of me! And then I turn around and see this guy up there screaming! This guy on fire screaming and flapping his arms like a demon! Like his hair is burning off his head and his clothes are going fast!

JERZY: Two bombers!

JAMES: What happened to them? Are they alive?

LITTLE J: The guy on fire might not make it. The other one was blown down the stairs. He's not doing too bad, they say.

ANNA LEE: We're going over there to check things out. Make a theater piece. It's a wild scene.

JAMES: Be careful. It's getting dangerous out there.

(The students rush out.)

JAMES: Watch your asses!

(The lighting now becomes strangely distorted. JAMES' reality is slipping out of focus.)

JAMES: It was finally happening, wasn't it? Barriers breaking down all over the place. All kinds of terrible things emerging from the darkness, making themselves violently known. Suddenly there seemed to be no price too horrible to pay. Because somehow we wanted it, needed it, didn't we? Were drawn to it. To get revenge, to gain validity, to move to the next level. To die trying.

(REGINE is sitting in her bedroom. She looks terrible. Her knees are pulled up to her chest; her clothes, for the first time, look unkempt, rumpled, slept in. JAMES walks into the room; she covers her eyes with her arm.)

JAMES: Why are you doing that, Regine, covering your face like that?

REGINE: I don't want to look at you.

JAMES: Fine, then don't.

(REGINE now raises both arms above her head and starts to scream. But the scream does not go very far; it is abruptly

*and weirdly cut off before it can be completed. Now her
hands go back to her face, covering her eyes.)*

JAMES: Where's Denny?

REGINE: He's over at Georgia's house.

JAMES: Fine. Then scream, scream your damned head
off, if you want.

*(Again she starts to scream, her hands raising above her
head, but once more the scream is cut off.)*

JAMES: Come on, Regine, come on! Give it another try!
Blow the roof off the goddamned place why not!

*(Her body convulses, her hands go up to her face again;
it sounds like she may be sobbing. Now she removes her
hands—her face strangely composed.)*

REGINE: So who is this woman that you're having
your affair with? Is she young, beautiful, smart? Or
maybe just some truck-stop whore, who's poetic soul
suddenly enticed you?

*(At this point SANDY appears in the shadows and begins
moving slowly around the periphery of the scene. REGINE
does not see her, but JAMES does, though he cannot bring
himself to look directly at her.)*

REGINE: So who is she, James?

JAMES: She teaches in the anthropology department.

REGINE: I didn't know that you knew anyone over
there.

JAMES: One day I just ran into her. That's all. It was an
accident. I mean, I just… *(He stops.)*

REGINE: So are you going to leave me for her?

(JAMES doesn't answer REGINE.)

REGINE: And how do you expect me to manage out
here in the middle of nowhere by myself? I barely
know a soul. Living alone, just me and Dennis—it

would be impossible! And I don't want to go back home either. My mother? If I have to go back to her it would be a disaster. I know I'd still hate her. But I don't know if it'd be with more or less intensity. The whole thing would be different, I'm sure. Confusing. Possibly overwhelming. *(Suddenly panicking)* And I'm not prepared, James! For any major life revisions! I've got all that I can possibly handle right now!

JAMES: Forget it. It'll be alright. *(Slight pause)* I was just confused. Momentarily confused.

REGINE: What do you mean?

JAMES: *(He is now looking directly at* SANDY.*)* She's nothing to me, this woman. Believe me. She was just there, happened to be there when I needed her. It was just…just a superficial…a physical attraction. Nothing more.

*(*SANDY *lights a cigarette.)*

JAMES: She just wasn't real to me.

*(*SANDY *goes over to the bed, puts her cigarette in an ashtray on the night table, then gets on top of the bed and begins jumping up and down.)*

JAMES: Not like here, with you and Denny. Not like our life together. Not like my commitment to you and Denny. Because that's where my goddamned reality is! That's where my real life is! Here with the two of you!

*(*SANDY*'s jumping grows faster.* REGINE *just stares at* JAMES.*)*

JAMES: Do you hear me? Do you hear what I'm saying, Regine?

REGINE: Do what you want, James. It's all the same to me.

JAMES: But you just said that, that you wanted, wanted us to—you said that you wanted me, that you wanted me, that you... *(He stops.)*

REGINE: What are you saying? It's your life, isn't it?

JAMES: *(Starting to come apart.)* Fuck you! Fuck you and what you're doing to me, Regine! Don't you see, don't you goddamn see what, what you're...what you're doing to.... *(Suddenly he stops, and pulls himself together.)* My reality is here, my responsibility; and that's all there is to it. I don't need anything else. I don't need anybody else. I can handle it. *(Now he turns and looks directly at SANDY.)* What else could I do? A coward like me!

REGINE: Whatever you have to do.

(SANDY flops down on the bed now and picks up the cigarette and takes a drag—aggressive, angry, sexual. REGINE coughs, then goes over to the window and looks out.)

(Suddenly SANDY grinds out the cigarette in the ashtray, gets to her feet, and begins to rip the bedclothes off the bed; now, with the sheet in her hands, she begins to rub it, violently, erotically, up and down her body, as if she were trying to reach orgasm, then suddenly, stopping in disgust, she throws it across the room. JAMES has been watching her. Now she looks directly at him, then getting off the bed, walks across the room and exits.)

REGINE: It's starting to rain out there.

(The lights fall on REGINE.)

(JAMES is now alone in the bedroom.)

JAMES: Something happened to Regine. Once, long ago, I think. I don't know what it was exactly. I never knew really. And she never told me. And I never knew how to ask. And I don't know how to help her. Even though I want to help her. Even though I try; or I think I try.

Something happened to Regine long before I ever met her, before I ever kissed her. And I never figured out how to make it disappear.

(Now the lights change. Time has passed. But JAMES *is still in the bedroom. He picks up the sheet that* SANDY *has thrown, and starts to wrap it around himself.)*

JAMES: Sandy, Sandy. It's been weeks since I've seen you, but I can't ask anyone, can't say: "Hey, by the way, have you seen, anybody seen, what's her name, that, that Sandra, yes, Sandra Townsend. What a pain in the ass she is, but has anybody…because I haven't seen her for a while." Sandy, Sandy… *(He pulls the sheet tighter around himself.)* We have this theory around here, called the Domino Theory: one falls, then the next, and then the next, etc. It's a highly respected theory, even a sacred theory, in some circles. A lot of young men are playing it these days, and losing. As the dominoes come crashing down upon them. *(Pause)* Sandy, Sandy.

(In the distance, we hear the whistle of the Red Train, and catch a glimpse of it crossing the prairie.)

JAMES: *(Crying out)* Sandy! Where are you? *(Except for his head, he has now wrapped himself completely in the sheet.)* And this is the way some of them come home. After playing dominoes.

*(*JAMES *now wraps his head. Darkness)*

(The lights come up on the three theatre students; gradually we see JAMES *in bed behind them, somewhat hidden in the shadows, still partially wrapped in the sheet, but with his head and upper body exposed.)*

ANNA LEE: It makes me sick just to think about it.

JERZY: *(Putting his arm around her)* I know, baby, I know. It's a major bummer.

ANNA LEE: I never liked her, but it's all so horrible.

LITTLE J: I never knew anybody murdered before.

JAMES: *(Sitting up on the bed)* What, What?

(They are not yet aware of him.)

ANNA LEE: I just heard, about ten minutes ago. What the hell happened?

LITTLE J: A farmer found her, I heard, or maybe it was a truck driver, everybody's saying something different. Anyway, she was in a cornfield, naked or almost naked. Maybe some pervert did it? Nobody seems to know much except that she's been killed. Poor girl.

JERZY: It's not right, stranguling a girl like that.

JAMES: What, what? *(He gets out of the bed now, with the sheet still half wrapped around him; now he goes over to them.)* What, what? Who was killed? Who?

ANNA LEE: That girl Sandy, Sandy Townsend. Somebody murdered her.

(ANNA LEE begins to tremble and cry a little. JERZY tries to comfort her. Now both JERZY and LITTLE J. begin to speak to JAMES, telling him what happened. But we can't hear what they're saying; we can only see their lips moving, and the astonishment and horror on JAMES' face. Now the lights begin to fade and the students exit together. JAMES remains where he was.)

JAMES: What, what? Who was killed? Some girl, was it? Sandra Townsend? No, I don't think so. Funny, but I don't remember what they said exactly. Tell me again: *(Crying out)* Who was killed? Who the fuck was killed?

(Now we see hear the whistle of the Red Train bearing down on JAMES. He doesn't move. Darkness)

(JAMES' office. JAMES and STONES are present. STONES is going through JAMES' books and papers, tossing them about, seemingly taking pleasure in the chaos he is creating.)

JAMES: You have no right to do this, detective.

STONES: I have all the blood-given right in the world.

JAMES: So you've now become the Angel, haven't you, Stones?

STONES: Let me tell you something about The Angel, what he said to me: they're all guilty, Sergeant Stones. The Gooks and the Americans. But some are more guilty than others. And those belong to you.

JAMES: So you must be very happy now, with your hands on me.

STONES: Take heart, it'll soon be over. (*He smiles. Then reaching behind some books on a bookshelf.*) Hey, what's this? (*He is holding a notebook.*) What could this be?

JAMES: Give that back, Stones!

(JAMES *tries to get the book, but* STONES *pulls away from. Now he starts reading.*)

STONES: This is interesting, very interesting. Really sick stuff.

JAMES: I entered into the heart of darkness, and wrote of the loss of love, and the love of loss; about the betrayal of love, and the nothingness of betrayal.

STONES: So, when did you write this, before or after you killed her?

(JAMES *starts to laugh.*)

STONES: Before or after, professor?

JAMES: (*He continues laughing, seemingly near the edge of collapse.*) After, after. I wrote it after.

STONES: It's alright, it's alright. I understand. Things could be worse, much worse, really. (*He now starts to become* JAMES—*his body and voice changing.*) Take a look at me. My life is coming apart. They follow me everywhere I go. My wife even, they're tailing her too. Bugging our phone. Watching our house with binoculars. Day and night. Even out with our son, on a family drive. We're not safe! Nothing sacred! They're right behind us! Never missing a trick.

JAMES: Stop it, Stones.

STONES: Prowling around my department. Talking to teachers, talking to students.

JAMES: You have no right to do this to me.

STONES: They have no right to do this to me. But inside my head it's even worse. She's there, you know, a ghost, a vampire. Sucking my heart's blood. She won't leave until I confess. But I can't do it. As hard as I try, I can't make it happen.

JAMES: What stops you?

STONES: My pride, my identity. Now all false, all empty. But I can't seem to let go.

JAMES: Try.

STONES: Yes, yes. (*He takes his wallet, his badge, and then his gun, putting each one on the desk in front of* JAMES. *He does this in a very slow, almost ritualistic manner.*) Now take them from me, brother. Free me from myself.

JAMES: Yes, I will. (*Slowly he picks up the gun and points it at* STONES.) Tell me, professor, is it loaded?

STONES: What do you think?

JAMES: Is it loaded, Fucking Ranger? Is it loaded?

STONES: What do you actually think?

JAMES: I think I'll have to try it!

(JAMES *continues pointing the gun at* STONES *for a few more seconds, then crying out, slams it down on the desk and exits. Darkness*)

(JAMES' *house.* JAMES *and* REGINE *are present.*)

REGINE: There were three of them here. This Detective Stones and two others. They went through everything, pulled everything apart. Dennis was terrified. They took a bunch of your things, put them in a bag and left. They had warrants. They were horrible.

JAMES: I'm sorry they came here.

REGINE: It was that girl, wasn't it, the murdered girl that you had your affair with, wasn't it?

JAMES: Yes.

REGINE: Did you kill her, James?

JAMES: *(He stares at her for a few moments.)* What's the difference?

REGINE: *What's* the difference? What does that mean, James?

JAMES: She's gone, isn't she? Never more to be… anymore.

REGINE: Tell me the truth: did you kill her?

JAMES: Where's Denny?

REGINE: He's out in the yard.

(JAMES *starts to exit.*)

REGINE: Don't go near him! Don't…

JAMES: Don't ever say that, Regine! Don't ever try and keep me away from my son! *(He exits.)*

REGINE: *(Softly)* Did you kill her, James?

(Darkness)

(Early evening. An underground parking lot in the university. HARRIS is present. He is quite drunk. There are a few bandages stuck on his face. He has just dropped his keys.)

HARRIS: Now where the hell are my keys? *(He pokes around with his foot looking for them.)* Gosh darn screwball keys. *(He leans over to get a better look, almost tips over, then getting his balance, straightens up.)* Oh, boy, whoopsy whoopsy! *(He laughs and takes a sip of his drink.)* What a life! What great times! Hey, where's my wallet? *(Pats his back pocket.)* There's my wallet. Wallet's fine. *(Laughs)* But, my gun? Where's my gun? *(He begins frantically patting his jacket pockets.)* Ahhh. There's my gun. Gun's just fine. Can't go out without your gun these days. *(Laughs, then looks at his drink.)* What a beautiful drink. *(He takes a sip.)* Best drink I've ever had in my entire life. The pleasure is still there. *(Now he begins to read the bumper stickers on the cars around him.)* BLACK POWER NOW, SEND OUR TROOPS HOME, LEGALIZE MARIJUANA, OPPRESSED PEOPLE UNITE. Oppressed people!—who the hell is more oppressed than me these days? *(He grasps the gun inside his jacket pocket.)* Blow them from here to hallelujah! Radical terrorists, drug addicted lunatics, mad bombers, homooo—sexuals, perverts of all kinds! Dirty hair, dirty feet, dirty minds, dirty ideas! Bam, bam, bam, bam, bam! And I want my mother back! Why the fuck did she have to die and leave me flat for! Mooootherrrrr! *(He looks down.)* Oh, there's my keys. {He reaches down to get them and falls flat on his face.}

(JAMES enters at the other side of the parking lot and sees HARRY lying there.)

JAMES: Harry, is that you?

HARRIS: What's left of me, anyway.

JAMES: Are you alright? Do you need a hand or something? *(He starts to walk towards him.)*

HARRIS: No! Stay where you are! I'm thinking! Have a little respect for the intellectual process and let me finish my thought. *(Slight pause)* There. Now it's complete. A perfectly formed thought. *(He struggles to his feet.)* You look good standing there like that, James.

JAMES: Like what, Harry?

HARRIS: Standing there with the light on you like that. Your vital organs exposed. I've seen men like that before, James. Quite a sight.

JAMES: So what was your thought, Harry, the one you just finished thinking?

HARRIS: That we must never be afraid to serve the goddess Justice, no matter what the cost. *(He pulls the gun out of his jacket and points it at* JAMES.) No matter what it takes.

JAMES: Hey, Harry, let's just cool it. Put the gun away, and then we can talk about justice all you want.

HARRIS: But I don't want to just talk about it, James. I want to live it! For it is this pure desire of mine that marks me as a man to be reckoned with—thus raising me above the howling animal masses that are presently gathering to destroy us! *(He fires at* JAMES *and misses.)*

*(*JAMES *starts running, trying to hide behind the cars, as* HARRIS *pursues him, his hand shaking, firing wildly.)*

HARRIS: You can run you, but you can't hide! Not from old Harry Harris! Professor Harris is going to send you back home to New York, all nice and comfy in your own body bag! *(He laughs.)*

(He fires his last shot as JAMES *runs out of the parking lot.)*

HARRIS: That's right, run, you little coward. But I'm still a'comin. I've got a pocket full of ammunition. I'll make it up that hill! Mow you all down! Japs, protesters, fornicators, whoever, whatever!

*(*HARRIS *is trying to reload his gun, as we hear the sound of sirens approaching the parking lot. A police car now enters, its lights shining on him. We now hear the* VOICE *of a police officer.)*

VOICE: Drop that gun! I said, drop that gun and put your hands up! I said, drop…

(HARRIS *drops the gun and puts his hands up.*)

HARRIS: But first, officer, I think you should know, that I'm a tenured professor here at the university, and also a decorated war hero. Now let me tell you exactly what transpired here this evening.

(*Darkness*)

(STONES' *office at the police station.* JAMES *and* STONES *are present.*)

JAMES: So Harris is out on bail.

STONES: That's what I said.

JAMES: Then I guess that nobody cares that he actually tried to kill me.

STONES: It was you, he said.

JAMES: What?

STONES: It was you stalking him, trying to kill him, he said. That's why he was armed. The old man is terrified of you.

JAMES: And why would I want to kill him?

STONES: Because he knows that you killed Sandra Townsend, that's why. She came to him and told him what was going on.

JAMES: What are you saying?

STONES: She told him that you were threatening to kill her!

JAMES: That's a lie! She may have told him something, but she didn't tell him that!

STONES: She told him that she had an affair with you. A brief affair. It only lasted a few weeks. A terrible mistake, she said. Because you became obsessed

with her and wouldn't let her break it off. Said YOU
WOULDN'T ALLOW IT! Said YOU'D KILL HER
FIRST! RAPE HER AND KILL HER if she ever tried to
LEAVE YOU!

JAMES: Then why didn't she go to the police, tell them
what I said, instead of going to Harris?

STONES: Because he's an old friend of the family,
someone she knew and loved and trusted ever since
she was a little kid.

JAMES: That's a lie! She knew him but she never loved
or trusted him. He's a twisted old bastard. A liar and
a drunk, and probably some kind of pervert. And she
knew it!

STONES: Whatever he is, he got up the courage to
face you down! And then you beat the shit out of
him, didn't you? Knocked him all over your office!
Loosened a couple of his teeth!

JAMES: I never touched him!

STONES: You beat the hell out of him! Look at his face.

JAMES: He did that to himself.

STONES: Attacked his own face! Give me a break! You
gave him a terrible beating. People heard him pleading
for his life in your office! Started carrying a gun around
because of you! And then he spots you laying for him
in the parking lot. A pipe or a hammer, or God knows
what, in your hand. Then all of a sudden, you're
coming at him! Screaming you're going to bash his
skull in! Of course he panics and opens fire! What the
hell did you expect him to do, invite you home for
cocktails?

JAMES: *(Starting to get up.)* Do me a favor, Stones, get
it over with. As fast as you can. Alright? Quickly,
quickly.

STONES: You could sit down with me, now, you know; I'll get some coffee; we'll work out a confession, no big deal; just tell me what really happened.

(JAMES *starts walking off into the shadows.*)

STONES: Think about your family, think about the agony you're causing your family. *(Suddenly, crying out...)* Think about me! What you're doing to me! The price I'm paying! Keep it up much more longer and I may be forced to do something the Angel forbids!

(Darkness. The lights come back up on JAMES' *house. He and* REGINE *are present. She has been packing.)*

REGINE: It's not fair, taking your classes away from you like that.

JAMES: I'm a murder suspect. What do you expect?

REGINE: Still, it's not right You'll drive us to the airport?

(JAMES *nods.*)

REGINE: I'm sorry for everything, James. I really am.

JAMES: So am I. Where's Denny?

REGINE: Out back. Saying goodbye to his friends.

(JAMES *starts to leave, then stops.*)

JAMES: You know, Regine, I always wanted to ask you something. Don't worry—it's not about your unhappiness.

REGINE: Then what is it?

JAMES: About your heart, Regine, what's really and truly in your heart?

REGINE: That's easy, James.

JAMES: Yes.

REGINE: My heart is in my heart. *(Pause)* Only my heart is in my heart. Nothing else.

JAMES: I understand. *(Pause)* I'm sorry, Regine. I really am.

REGINE: So am I, James.

(JAMES exits. Darkness. The lights come back up on his bedroom. It is even more dishevelled than it was when we last saw it. He sits on the edge of the bed, staring off into the distance; LITTLE J. is standing alone stage left; he is moving slowly, hypnotically to a kind of Indian raga-rock; JERZY and ANNA LEE are stage right, hands locked tight around each other, staring deep into one another's eyes, their bodies swaying.)

(The lights come up brighter on JERZY and ANNA LEE; they seem totally stoned.)

ANNA LEE: Tell me about Cracow, Jerzy!

JERZY: It is God's biggest, most lunatic fucking mistake! But still, it's light glistens like diamonds, like the tears falling from the eyes of the twenty seven million tragic angels flying like maniacs, that God-bleeding night, high above the Garden of Gethsemane.

ANNA LEE: Take me there, Jerzy! Take me to Cracow now!

JERZY: Yes, Mary Magdalene, yes, yes!

ANNA LEE: Now, Jerzy, now!

(They fall to the ground in a mad erotic embrace. The music grows louder, the light dips into darkness, then comes back up on JAMES, encasing him in a sphere of darkness and fire. Now ANNA LEE appears at the edge of the fire, looking like some lunatic angel.)

ANNA LEE: How can there be laughter, how can there be pleasure, when your world is being destroyed? When you are in deep darkness, will you not ask for a lamp?

JAMES: Yes, Anna Lee, yes.

ANNA LEE: Teachings of the Buddha.

JAMES: Yes, Anna Lee, yes. *(He is looking out into the fiery darkness now, looking for a lamp, crying out...)* Sandy! Sandy!

(The music increases; darkness; now the lights come back up. The three students have now become a chorus of tragic angels surrounding JAMES.*)*

THE MEN: Run, Ranger, run! Run from the police, run from yourself, run from death! Run, Ranger, run!

ANNA LEE: He can't. He can't.

THE MEN: Into your black Mustang, Ranger. Drive into the sun! Anywhere but here! Anywhere but here!

ANNA LEE: He can't. He won't. He must stay here.

THE MEN: Why, why must he stay?

ANNA LEE: To catch the killer; to free his soul.

(The music rises, darkness. The lights come up; a similar mixture of burning and darkness. ANNA LEE *is sitting on the bed with* JAMES. *We can no longer see either* LITTLE J *or* JERZY.*)*

JAMES: I killed her.

ANNA LEE: Did you?

JAMES: Yes. Like this.

*(*JAMES *puts his hands around* ANNA LEE's *neck and begins to apply pressure. After a few moments, he let's go.)*

JAMES: See, it's easy. It was so easy.

ANNA LEE: Why'd you kill her, Ranger?

JAMES: For the war, because of the war. She believed in the war, but I didn't. I was a pacifist; so I killed her. *(He laughs.)*

ANNA LEE: No.

JAMES: Because I loved her; and sooner or later I knew that I would have become like her; so I killed her. *(He begins to laugh, then suddenly seems on the verge of tears.)* It was easy! Nobody knows for sure that I did it; even her spirit doesn't know for sure. *(He laughs a little.)* Only Stones; he seems to know. Because he speaks to God.

ANNA LEE: No, he doesn't.

JAMES: I'm going to tell Stones. He wants me to sign a confession. Then her spirit will know and she'll be able to rest.

ANNA LEE: No, James. Don't do it.

(The lights dip and come back up. STONES is now present, going about the room, gathering "evidence." LITTLE J is on one side of the room, moving to the music; ANNA LEE and JERZY on the other side of the room, moving slowly around each other. STONES doesn't see them, only JAMES, who is sitting on the bed.)

STONES: *(Picking up invisible objects with a tweezers, then putting them into a bag.)* A forgotten thought. A map of blood. A speck of evil. A drop of venom. An unheard noise. *(Checking out a table)* The blueprint of a plan. The outline of rage. The shape of murder.

JAMES: Detective Stones?

STONES: What? Are you speaking to me?

JAMES: I want to tell you something.

STONES: Something important, perhaps?

JAMES: Yes, very important. I wanted to tell you, that I, that I kil kil…

(ANNA LEE moves quickly, clapping her hand over JAMES's mouth, smothering the word. STONES cannot see her.)

STONES: What? What's that? What did you say? Speak your mind. You said, you kil kil. Who'd you kill, mister? Huh? Spell it out. Names, methods, dates. I'm a professional. It's the complete atrocity I'm after. *(He waits for a reply, then turns away, seemingly bored with the whole matter.)* Ahh, who cares. Sooner or later you'll discover the right words, and then you'll speak them out, won't you, brother? Loud and clear, for me to hear. Of course, you will. I have great faith in you.

(Now STONES *takes out a camera and begins snapping pictures of* JAMES *and the room. The camera produces a blinding flash.* JAMES *hides his face. Now* STONES *disappears into the darkness.* ANNA LEE *takes* JAMES *in her arms.)*

ANNA LEE: Good, James. You did good. I'm proud of you. *(She kisses him gently on the lips.)*

(Darkness. The lights come up. Some daylight now. JAMES *is now a few steps removed from the bedroom, standing with* JERZY *and* ANNA LEE, *who have somehow been able to coax him outside.)*

JERZY: It is all so strange, all of this wildass America to me.

JAMES: What do you mean?

JERZY: People here, how crazy they behave. What can you really know? What seems like it is, so often is not. Like you. Did we know how much you ever loved her? No way. We thought that you hated her right wing guts. Now we see this is really a complete tragedy for you. Everything's confused. Take Little J, as another for example.

*(*ANNA LEE *shoots him a look.* JERZY *notices it.)*

JERZY: Hey, is there some unexplained reason for not speaking now?

JAMES: What are you saying, Jerzy?

ANNA LEE: Nothing important.

JERZY: That we never knew that he was this close and secret friend of poor Sandra.

ANNA LEE: Why'd you have to say that for? We promised Little J. that we'd never tell anybody, didn't we?

JERZY: Well, I just thought...

ANNA LEE: In America we try and keep our promises, Jerzy.

JERZY: Things were different those times, with the poor girl being still alive.

JAMES: Could you please tell me what's going on, Anna Lee?

ANNA LEE: Oh, somehow Little J and Sandy became these very close friends; but he swore us never to tell anyone, especially you, because he thought it would completely blow his radical credentials, and you might kick him out of the theater group.

JAMES: That's weird. How did they become friends?

ANNA LEE: His brother was a war hero, you know, killed in Vietnam.

JAMES: I didn't even know he had a brother.

ANNA LEE: He was in the Special Forces or something; was over there two or three times; got a bunch of medals; I think he wanted to talk to her about him, things that he couldn't tell the rest of us, I guess.

JERZY: He loved her, you know.

JAMES: Loved her?

ANNA LEE: A lot. Said she was like a sister to him, that he could tell her anything and that she would always understand.

JERZY: And you too were like his lost brother, he once said, in deep confidence.

JAMES: Loved her? He loved her. That's what you said, isn't it?

ANNA LEE: Yes, he loved her very much.

(JAMES *walks off into the shadows. Darkness*)

(*The lights come back up.* JAMES *is now in* LITTLE J*'s house, standing in the shadows, waiting for him to come home. After a few moments, the door opens, and* LITTLE J *enters.* JAMES *steps into the light, startling* LITTLE J.)

LITTLE J: Holy smokes, Teach! What's happening! What the hell are you doing here? You scared the hell out of me, man. (*He laughs.*)

(*Silence*)

JAMES: Why'd you do it, Little J.?

LITTLE J: (*Laughing.*) Oh, man! The things that go through my mind when people ask me stuff like that! Wowwwww!

JAMES: Stuff like what, Little J.?

LITTLE J: Stuff concerning all the crazy "its" I've done all my life. It seems someone is always asking me about them lately.

JAMES: And now it's me, doing the asking. Isn't it, Little J?

LITTLE J: All my life, I guess I wanted to reach the truth—not in just some intellectual, or abstract kind of way—but to totally and completely experience it.

JAMES: And how do you manage to do that, Little J.?

LITTLE J: By risking myself. Because if the risk is big enough, then the knowledge you emerge with just might change your life forever.

JAMES: So did killing Sandra Townsend do that for you, Little J., change your life forever?

LITTLE J: *(Laughing)* Ho-ly shit! Hey, Fucking Ranger, who've you been talking to, man? Too much time locked in the old hacienda with the hippies, I'd say.

JAMES: It had something to do with your brother, didn't it?

LITTLE J: What? What are you saying?

JAMES: Sandy was a patriot, the daughter of a very patriotic family, a military family; people like that sent your brother to Vietnam, didn't they, sent him there to be killed?

LITTLE J: Hey, let's keep our hands off my brother. I mean, who really wants to talk about him with a sneaky little draft dodger like you.

JAMES: What did you call me?

LITTLE J: Hey, don't take me seriously, Teach, I'm just being an asshole.

JAMES: I never dodged the draft, Little J.

LITTLE J: All you guys who hate the war: protesters, radicals, draft dodgers, whatever you want to call yourselves—what have you accomplished; who have you ever really saved? So go home and be proud, but leave me the hell out of it.

JAMES: We didn't save your brother, did we, Little J?

LITTLE J: None of you helped him. Nobody. *(Slight pause)* But I'll tell you, she made me feel good, about him. I couldn't talk to anyone else, could I? But she made me feel proud about him. That's why we became secret friends.

JAMES: But what made you decide to kill her, Little J.?

LITTLE J: What it really is, people like her, I'm talking about, what they really want, what makes them feel really good, is bodies, lots of dead bodies with medals pinned on them; and fancy military funerals with lots of guns going off. Makes them cry, gives them shivers, makes them feel super American or something. But all I ever wanted was my brother. My father was never anything to us—a spiteful, loud mouthed bastard—I'm glad he finally left. But my brother was the real thing: an outrageous, roller coaster, stand-up kind of guy! And she killed him! Maybe not personally; but it was definitely her lineage, her mind-set that did it. It was weird, because even when she was making me feel good about the great things he stood for, I was hating her; because it was those thoughts, those ideas that killed him. But mainly I was hating myself for needing her the way I did. That was really the worst of it. What I felt about myself. Because I couldn't stand myself anymore. Or make any sense of my life.

JAMES: I loved her, Little J.

LITTLE J: Good! Now you know what I feel! Now you have a sacred grave to visit, like I do!

(JAMES *starts moving towards him.* LITTLE J *backs away from him.*)

LITTLE J: I'm not afraid of you. I mean, the truth is, I didn't kill anybody. I'm just telling you about my secret friendship with Sandra Townsend.

JAMES: I loved her more than anyone, Little J.

LITTLE J: Good, good. Because you asked for it! You're not a stand up guy! You didn't live up to your beliefs like my brother! I was mistaken about you! You had no reason to get involved with her! And now you've got what you deserve. Both of you!

(JAMES *rushes at him.* LITTLE J *throws a chair in his way.*)

LITTLE J: I'm not afraid of you! But, but… (*Suddenly he seems lost, confused, looking wildly about him…*) You know what it was: I was feeling really bad that night when I ran into her. "Hey come on, Little J., cheer up;

let's go for a ride." And we got in my car and drove
around for a while, ending up out in the cornfields;
and by then I was crying and she was trying to comfort
me—but in my mind I knew that it couldn't go on
anymore. You see, I had these thoughts, thoughts that
I couldn't admit that I'd ever thought, but were still
thought. And could not be taken back. And suddenly
they were controlling me.

JAMES: Thoughts about killing her.

LITTLE J: Both of you, really.

JAMES: What?

LITTLE J: You see, she had told me about the two of
you, what had happened between you. I couldn't
believe it! The two of you! It was unbelievable! I felt so
fucking betrayed! I can't explain it. Maybe if I hadn't
known, maybe... (*He trails off.*)

JAMES: But you did know. And suddenly you had us
both, didn't you, Little J?

LITTLE J: (*Smiling at him*) Yes, I did. And then I saw her
face in the moonlight smiling at me—and suddenly
I knew that I was totally serious, with this piece of
rope stashed under the front seat.... And that I had to
kill her! To make her into a sacrifice! Because she was
beautiful! And I loved her! But I knew that everyone
had to pay for this war! And the best way to pay, is
with what you love! So I strangled her. And then I
dragged her body out into the fields, and pulled off
her clothes, so that the moonlight would fall on her
nakedness, and the world could see the terrible and
beautiful thing that I'd done.

(JAMES *leaps on him. Darkness. There is a struggle.*
The lights come back up. Music from the Le Sacre du
Printemps, *the* Second Part, The Sacrifice, *is playing*

loudly. LITTLE J *is in a chair, with* JAMES *standing behind him, a rope around his neck, slowly strangling him.)*

JAMES: *(Calmly)* Lucky, lucky, Little J. because you're experiencing the ultimate risk now, the ultimate trip. Aren't you? Death, Little J, death! *(He stops tightening the rope.)* Are you?

LITTLE J: *(Barely able to speak)* Yes. Because...I did... what I believed. Not...like...you.

JAMES: Good. That's just what I like. A man with convictions! *(He begins tightening the rope again; this time with some fury.)*

(The volume of the music is growing steadily louder.)

*(*SANDY *now appears in the room.* JAMES *sees her; startled...)*

JAMES: Sandy! Why are you here? You shouldn't be here. Go away, go away, Sandy!

SANDY: I can't, Jimmy.

JAMES: You shouldn't be here watching me! GET OUT OF HERE!

SANDY: Don't strangle him, Jimmy.

JAMES: Yes. Yes, I am!

*(*JAMES *applies more pressure.* LITTLE J's *body begins to thrash.)*

JAMES: You can't stop me!

SANDY: No, Jimmy, no! I don't want you to do it!

(Time is frozen; the volume all the way up. Now JAMES *stops strangling him, his hands relaxing a little, but with the rope still wound tight around* LITTLE J's *neck.)*

JAMES: Sandy, please, let me finish what I'm doing. I don't want you here! I don't want you to see what I'm doing!

SANDY: There's been enough killing, don't you think?

JAMES: As soon as this one is over.

(JAMES *starts to tighten the rope;* LITTLE J *struggles.* SANDY *starts moving towards* JAMES, *her hand extended, as if to touch him.*)

SANDY: I think he's been broken enough. Don't you, Jimmy?

JAMES: Not nearly enough! *(Softly)* He took everything from me.

SANDY: No.

JAMES: What do you mean *no?* You're gone, aren't you? Taken from me. And he did it! He killed you!

SANDY: It's not over.

JAMES: How can you say that?

SANDY: Because it's not.

(JAMES *wonders what* SANDY *means. His hands fall to his side.* LITTLE J. *doesn't move.*)

JAMES: I reviled you! I cursed and reviled you!

SANDY: And I reviled you!

JAMES: And I murdered you! He was right. Both of us did it! First I'll take care of him, and then I'll, I'll....

(*Once more he starts tightening the rope;* LITTLE J *begins to thrash violently.*)

SANDY: No! He wasn't right! You didn't murder me! No! Stop, James, stop now! Stooopppppp!

JAMES: I have to.

SANDY: Don't make become angry with you! Don't make me furious with you! Don't make me hate you, James! Stop killing him now! Stop it! Or I'll turn from you forever! I swear! Forever, Jimmy! Forever!

(JAMES *stops strangling* LITTLE J; *and then throws himself wildly about the room, crying out, crashing into things…*)

JAMES: Aaaaaaa! I had him! Aaaaaaa! Just a few more seconds! I could have done it! I could have killed him! Why didn't you let me finish him!?!

SANDY: Just look at him, James. Just look at him.

(SANDY *goes over to him and touches* LITTLE J'*s face. For the first time he sees her and begins to sob, trying to push her away, trying to hide from her.*)

SANDY: Shhhhh, shhhhhh. You'll be alright. You're alright now. Look at your hair. What a mess. (*She begins to fix his hair.*) You'll be alright. Quiet down, Little J. It's all over now. Nobody will hurt you.

(LITTLE J *closes his eyes.*)

SANDY: Yes, yes. That's good, that's good.

JAMES: It was wrong to save him.

SANDY: Let it go, Jimmy. Let him go. Let it all go.

JAMES: How can I?

SANDY: Give it a chance.

(*The sound of the Red Train is heard in the distance.*)

JAMES: But it's not all gone. There's the train, the Red Train again.

SANDY: But it's far away, Jimmy, far away this time. And each time it will be further and further away. You'll see.

JAMES: It'll go away; but it won't be gone.

SANDY: But things will change, James. And that's what's important. You'll see, you'll see.

(*The lights change;* SANDY *begins to fade into the brightness, into the darkness.* JAMES *watches her.*)

JAMES: *(Softly)* Sandy, don't go. Not yet. Please. Stay for a while. Fix my hair too, Sandy. It's all mussed up.

(Darkness. The lights come up. JAMES *is still present.* STONES *is on stage now, handcuffing* LITTLE J. *He is about to lead him off, when he suddenly turns towards* JAMES…)

STONES: This is not the one I wanted.

JAMES: Because he's not one of the guiltiest, is he, Stones? He's just another poor victim.

STONES: A loser. Some cast off lunatic. I've wasted my time.

JAMES: So keep looking, Stones. And sooner or later, you'll find him. The guiltiest one. The one you really want. But first, I'm afraid, you'll have to go back to that killing ground of yours. The last man standing! He's the one you want, Stones! He's your man! The one you've been looking for all along! Get your hands on him, and you'll be in the money, detective.

STONES: *(Suddenly coming apart)* No. I can't. I, I… not back…not back there. I, I… *(Getting control of himself)* No! You're wrong! Because there's no last man standing! You see, I lied to you. There were no survivors! None at all. They're all dead, New York! Every single one of them is dead! Every single one of them killed that day! And nobody misses them, which is the strange part. Nobody cares. Nobody gives a damn. The erasure being complete. The wipe out being total.

(Now STONES *exits, leading* LITTLE J *into the darkness.)*

(Darkness. The lights come up. Late afternoon. JAMES *is alone in the cornfields. A barn is behind him. He stands there quietly for a few moments; now we hear the sound of the animals.)*

JAMES: I think I could turn and live with animals, they are so placid and self-contained, I stand and look at them long and long.

(SANDY *now appears standing behind him.*)

JAMES: They do not sweat and whine about their condition, They do not lie awake in the dark and weep for their sins...

SANDY: And some of them were my best friends.

JAMES: *(Starting to turn around)* Sandy!

SANDY: Don't turn around. No need to. Just look at this beautiful day. This place. Take it in, Jimmy. It's yours.

JAMES: Yes, I will, Sandy. This beautiful place.

SANDY: How's Harry, by the way?

JAMES: He's in an asylum now, the madhouse, really. He went too far, it seems; he went completely around the bend of his last great bender. They don't think they can get him back; alcohol finally did its work, I suppose.

SANDY: Poor guy.

JAMES: I went to see him. He tried to kiss my hands; talked about all the great times we had, our fabulous discussions together. He knows that he's insane, though; he's terrified of it, but somehow accepts it. He thought it was night; it was blazing day. He sees rapacious animals hiding in the foliage, birds of prey in the sky. He thinks God cursed him on a Jap beach, through the half destroyed face of a dead Marine; the jaws began to jabber, he said, God's words pouring forth, cursing him, damning him to hell. He doesn't know why, what he did wrong; why God grew so angry with him? He began to sob. All he ever did was try to be a good soldier, he said. He thinks you're his daughter.

SANDY: He'll die soon. Peacefully.

JAMES: Oh, Sandy, how do you know that? Where are you now that you can know such things. *(He is about to turn around, to look at her, to go to her.)*

SANDY: No! It's alright, James. Stay where you are. Everything's as it should be. Everything will be fine. Because we were fine, James. we were miraculous. And we still are, beautiful and miraculous. No kidding. It's real; it's true. I'll always be excited about you. I'm telling you the truth. And please don't do anything foolish, like go out of your way to lead some kind of terrible life. Promise me that.

JAMES: I promise you.

SANDY: I couldn't stand that. Because…listen, listen, James…
We won't die! We don't die!
We can't!
We will not be swept away.
Nothing can obliterate us.
As we are the pure urge of the world,
Brought deathless and astonished,
Alive into each other's arms.
Are you hearing me, James?

JAMES: Yes. I am, Sandy.

SANDY: Lucky newborn babes!
Brought to life by the mad joy of our desires!
Wrapped as we were in the light
And the darkness of each other.
Holding tight before the endless flow,
Skies and prairies.
The wind like a bird in the barn above us.
Even war could not obliterate us!

JAMES: Then let me go with you, Sandy!

SANDY: No, James, no.
Let it go, let it go.
That's all it takes.
You'll see.

JAMES: I don't know if I can.

SANDY: You can; you will.
Everything is fine.
Trust me.
I'll never leave you.
I'll never leave you.

JAMES: I'll try, I will.
If you want me to.

SANDY: I do. I really do, James—because,
Listen: it's not so hard to understand, really;
Easier to understand than one ever imagined,
Though unexpected in every way.
And so soft, so soft with the light
Forever falling and gaining upon you,
Carrying you forward
Into endless birdsung mornings.
And so kind,
Allowing you to carry all that is important—
Every atom, every dream,
Every tenderness shared,
The breath, the motion,
The bloodbeat and the generosity of the other—
As it was truly felt, as it continues to be felt.

And soon it will be night, James,
With the darkness pressing us close together—
Closer than ever, somehow I know—
Our secrets and most tender thoughts mingling.
Oh, naked burning night…
My love, my love! Burning through me…

JAMES: Sandy…

SANDY: Don't say anything;
It's time, it's time.
As we were so lucky, James!
Given to love by those who loved us!
Taught to forgive by those who protected us!
I won't be contained!
I cannot be,
Brought to understanding as I have by you!

JAMES: No, It was you, Sandy!
It was you!
It was you who did it all!

SANDY: Don't say goodbye.
You don't have to.

JAMES: I know.

(She disappears into the light. We hear the sound of the animals, then the great deep, throbbing sound of the insects. Evening comes on, then night. The sky cascading with light and stars. JAMES hasn't moved.)

JAMES: I know, Sandy, I know.
I always knew, I always knew…

(His lips moving as he continues to whisper to the night, to the shape of her soul as it is revealed to him in the light and darkness of the heavens.)

END OF PLAY